DISEASES & DISORDERS

Anorexia
and
Bulimia

DISEASES & DISORDERS

Anorexia
and
Bulimia

Elizabeth Silverthorne

LUCENT BOOKS
A part of Gale, Cengage Learning

GALE
CENGAGE Learning

Detroit • New York • San Francisco • New Haven, Conn • Waterville, Maine • London

LIBRARY OF CONGRESS CATALOGING-IN-PUBLICATION DATA

Silverthorne, Elizabeth, 1930–
    Anorexia and bulimia / by Elizabeth Silverthorne.
        p. cm. -- (Diseases and disorders)
    Includes bibliographical references and index.
    ISBN 978-1-4205-0141-4 (hardcover)
    1. Eating disorders--Juvenile literature. 2. Bulimia--Juvenile literature. 3. Anorexia nervosa--Juvenile literature. I. Title.
    RC552.E18S557 2009
    616.85'26--dc22

                                                        2009022641

Lucent Books
27500 Drake Rd.
Farmington Hills, MI 48331

ISBN-13: 978-1-4205-0141-4
ISBN-10: 1-4205-0141-0

Printed in the United States of America
2 3 4 5 6 7 13 12 11 10 09

Printed by Bang Printing, Brainerd, MN 2nd Ptg., 12/2009

Table of Contents

"The Most Difficult Puzzles Ever Devised"

Charles Best, one of the pioneers in the search for a cure for diabetes, once explained what it is about medical research that intrigued him so. "It's not just the gratification of knowing one is helping people," he confided, "although that probably is a more heroic and selfless motivation. Those feelings may enter in, but truly, what I find best is the feeling of going toe to toe with nature, of trying to solve the most difficult puzzles ever devised. The answers are there somewhere, those keys that will solve the puzzle and make the patient well. But how will those keys be found?"

Since the dawn of civilization, nothing has so puzzled people—and often frightened them, as well—as the onset of illness in a body or mind that had seemed healthy before. A seizure, the inability of a heart to pump, the sudden deterioration of muscle tone in a small child—being unable to reverse such conditions or even to understand why they occur was unspeakably frustrating to healers. Even before there were names for such conditions, even before they were understood at all, each was a reminder of how complex the human body was, and how vulnerable.

While our grappling with understanding diseases has been frustrating at times, it has also provided some of humankind's most heroic accomplishments. Alexander Fleming's accidental discovery in 1928 of a mold that could be turned into penicillin has resulted in the saving of untold millions of lives. The isolation of the enzyme insulin has reversed what was once a death sentence for anyone with diabetes. There have been great strides in combating conditions for which there is not yet a cure, too. Medicines can help AIDS patients live longer, diagnostic tools such as mammography and ultrasounds can help doctors find tumors while they are treatable, and laser surgery techniques have made the most intricate, minute operations routine.

This "toe-to-toe" competition with diseases and disorders is even more remarkable when seen in a historical continuum. An astonishing amount of progress has been made in a very short time. Just two hundred years ago, the existence of germs as a cause of some diseases was unknown. In fact, it was less than 150 years ago that a British surgeon named Joseph Lister had difficulty persuading his fellow doctors that washing their hands before delivering a baby might increase the chances of a healthy delivery (especially if they had just attended to a diseased patient)!

Each book in Lucent's Diseases and Disorders series explores a disease or disorder and the knowledge that has been accumulated (or discarded) by doctors through the years. Each book also examines the tools used for pinpointing a diagnosis, as well as the various means that are used to treat or cure a disease. Finally, new ideas are presented—techniques or medicines that may be on the horizon.

Frustration and disappointment are still part of medicine, for not every disease or condition can be cured or prevented. But the limitations of knowledge are being pushed outward constantly; the "most difficult puzzles ever devised" are finding challengers every day.

Battling Anorexia and Bulimia

Most people find eating a natural, enjoyable activity. For an alarming number, however, it is a daily ordeal filled with pain and suffering. Millions of people are excessively concerned with food and weight and body shape. Instead of looking forward to their next meal with pleasure, they literally starve themselves or eat uncontrollably only to make themselves throw up. Only recently have these obsessions with food been recognized as eating disorders and treated as potentially deadly illnesses.

Anorexia

Aimee Liu has written two books about her struggles with eating disorders. In the first book, *Solitaire*, she does not name her obsession because she did not know it had a name. In this book she describes her early years as idyllic. When she was three and her brother Scott was eleven, the family moved to Delhi, India. Her father worked for the United Nations Documentary Film Department. Delhi was filled with contrasts: emerald gardens with shooting fountains, lakes filled with water lilies, and bejeweled temples along with snake charmers, sacred cattle on the sidewalks, and thousands of beggars sleeping in the streets.

Like other westerners living in India the Liu family had servants to take care of every need. These included a cook, a gardener, cleaners, sweepers, ayahs (nursemaids), and governesses. Aimee was healthy, safe, and well cared for. Two years later when the family returned to America, they moved into a home in Glenridge, Connecticut. Aimee felt like an alien in the new setting. She had a hard time relating to the children and teachers who were so different from those she had known in India.

Aimee was highly intelligent, though, and she learned to adapt—at least on the outside. Her brother Scott remained her best friend and ally. She could always tell him her problems and trust him to be helpful and sympathetic. But Scott was eight years older than she, and just as she was entering puberty he became engaged to be married. Aimee was devastated. Her best friend would no longer be on hand to reassure her daily that she was good-looking and worthwhile no matter what anyone else thought of her.

Despite being an excellent student with top grades, Aimee lacked self-confidence in her social relationships. Her teachers

Most people find eating a meal with friends and family enjoyable, but for those with an eating disorder this is a dreaded activity.

and parents praised her good work, but she longed to be more popular with her classmates. Perhaps, she decided, changing her appearance would help. When her grandmother referred to her as "chubby," and her mother said she could stand to lose a few pounds, Aimee knew what she wanted to do.

She asked for diet books and a scale for Christmas. She began to diet and exercise strenuously. Losing weight became the most important thing in her life. It dominated her thoughts until it became an obsession. When she found herself admired and envied by her classmates for her super thinness, she worked even harder at finding new ways to lose weight.

At fifteen, Aimee was accepted by Wilhelmina, a world-class modeling agency. She was on the cover of *American Girl* and featured in *Seventeen, Coed,* and *Ingénue.* This success, however, did not stop her compulsion to lose even more weight. By the time she was seventeen she had become so rail thin she could not fit into the clothes she was supposed to showcase. And her career as a model was over.

Her acceptance of herself and recovery from her compulsive behavior began while she attended Yale University. Encouraged by friends she made there, she began eating more normally and reached a healthy weight. She married and had two children. She thought her eating disorder problems were over.

Then problems in her marriage triggered a relapse. True to her scholarly nature, Liu began an in-depth study and research into eating disorders and wrote a book on the subject, called *Gaining.* In 2008 it was on the *New York Times* best seller list of nonfiction books. It has been highly praised by medical experts for its insights into the confusing and often misinterpreted diseases known as eating disorders. It also shows that anorexia is far more widespread than conventional wisdom indicates. Among its victims, Liu reveals, are not just rich, young white women, but also men, women, and children of all classes and races.

Bulimia

Perhaps the second most common eating disorder is bulimia. People who suffer from bulimia have many of the same traits as those who are diagnosed as being anorexic. They are often perfectionists who use their body weight and shape as a way of measuring their success in coping with their problems. The histories of many bulimics show that this is true even after they have achieved outstanding success in the eyes of the world.

Paula Abdul was a popular singer, songwriter, dancer, and choreographer in the 1980s and 1990s. Then she became a popular judge on the TV show *American Idol*. When she was in high school she seemed to have it all. She was class president,

Paula Abdul, singer, dancer, and judge on *American Idol*, became bulimic during adolescence.

a top honor student, and head cheerleader. At 5 feet 2 inches (157cm) she weighed between 105 and 110 pounds (between 47kg and 49kg). She thought she was too short and too heavy. She always wanted to be perfect and longed to be tall and skinny like other dancers she admired.

Abdul's bulimia began when she was an adolescent—gorging on food and then purging it from her body to keep from gaining weight. She describes her eating disorder as being "like war on my body. Me and my body have been on two separate sides. We've never, until recently, been on the same side."[1] She underwent extensive therapy at a clinic in Oklahoma and feels she has finally learned to deal with her bulimia. She is now a spokesperson for the National Eating Disorders Association (NEDA).

People with eating disorders often hide their obsession for many years by using various tricks and lying to family, friends, and doctors about their problems. Liu and Abdul are examples of courageous victims of eating disorders who are speaking out about their past struggles with these diseases. They hope to encourage other victims to take the scary but necessary steps to seek help before it is too late.

CHAPTER ONE

What Are Eating Disorders?

The more scientists discover about eating disorders, the more difficulty they have putting them in neatly labeled pigeonholes. The Alliance for Eating Disorders Awareness defines eating disorders as "eating habits that are hurtful to an individual: at times resulting in death."[2] A patient who begins as an anorexic may become bulimic. Either anorexics or bulimics may be bingers at times. Bingers may become anorexic and/or bulimic. As more information about the behavior of eating disorder victims comes to light, predicting who will have which disease is more difficult. Certain symptoms and habits, however, are characteristic of different eating disorders. And, fortunately, public and private victims are coming forward to share their experiences and thus help with the understanding of these puzzling diseases.

Who Has an Eating Disorder?

Eating disorders are marked by extremes in eating behavior. People with eating disorders may reduce their food intake to the point of starvation. Or they may eat huge amounts of food and then use extreme measures to try to rid their bodies of every calorie they have eaten. Or they may simply binge on food and become dangerously obese.

Binge eaters typically eat large quantities of food in a short time, eat when not hungry, and eat in secret.

The National Institute of Mental Health lists anorexia nervosa and bulimia nervosa as the two most deadly eating disorders. Binge eating disorder is a third potentially dangerous disease.

Eating disorder victims often try to hide their disease or claim their symptoms (such as extreme thinness) arise from some other cause. This behavior makes it impossible to know exactly how many people are suffering from eating disorders, or at what age they first developed symptoms, or how they are being affected by them. Data from reliable sources, however, show that despite growing awareness of the seriousness of these diseases, the number of victims is increasing.

In fact, experts agree that eating disorders have reached epidemic levels in America. ANAD (National Association of Anorexia Nervosa and Associated Disorders) says: "All segments of society are affected: Men and women, young and old,

Meanings

Anorexia means "loss of appetite." But that is not what actually happens. At the start of the disease people suffering from anorexia are extremely hungry most of the time and yet refuse to eat. They have not lost their appetite; they are simply overriding it.

Bulimia means "ox-hunger." That is a fairly good description because bulimics eat huge amounts of food (whether they are hungry or not).

Binge meant going on a drinking spree to most people thirty years ago. It still has that meaning, but today dictionaries add the meaning of "unrestrained indulgence." In everyday jargon, people who occasionally eat more than normal might say they "binged" on ice cream or potato chips. When eating disorders experts use the term *binge* they are usually referring to the eating patterns of patients who eat large amounts of food and have a feeling of loss of control.

rich and poor, all ethnicities, all socio-economic levels."[3] And ANAD estimates that 6 percent of people with serious eating disorders die.

Other reliable sources support the disturbing fact that eating disorders are widespread and growing. NEDA (National Eating Disorders Association) reports: "In the United States, as many as 10 million females and 1 million males are fighting a life and death battle with an eating disorder such as anorexia or bulimia. Millions more are struggling with binge eating disorder."[4] NEDA says that the peak onset of eating disorders occurs during puberty and the late teen/early adult years but adds that symptoms can occur as young as kindergarten.

The Alliance for Eating Disorders Awareness is a nonprofit organization that tracks eating disorders. It states that eating disorders "currently affect 24 million Americans, in which approximately 10–15% are men. In addition approximately 70 million individuals worldwide struggle with these disorders."[5]

Binge Eating

In addition to anorexia and bulimia, authorities rank binge eating disorder (BED) as a dangerous disease. Until recently BED was known as compulsive overeating—an apt name since the person temporarily loses control of his or her ability to stop eating. Binge eating is often associated with depression.

Not all binge eaters are overweight. Some, however become seriously obese—a condition that can lead to life-threatening health problems. These health risks are similar to those associated with clinical obesity and, according to NEDA, include:

- High blood pressure
- High cholesterol levels
- Heart disease
- Diabetes mellitus
- Gallbladder disease[6]

Binge eaters characteristically eat large quantities of food in short periods of time, eat when not hungry, eat in secret, and feel distress and guilt over their behavior despite feeling unable to control it.

Binge eating is often associated with depression. Binge eaters feel distress and guilt over their behavior despite feeling unable to control it.

Christopher G. Fairburn, a specialist in treating binge eating disorder, describes the aftermath of a binge:

Those who binge may say they experience some immediate, though temporary positive feelings. For example, they may feel a sense of relief. Feelings of hunger and deprivation will have disappeared, and perhaps the depression or anxiety that may have triggered the binge has been displaced. But these positive effects are soon replaced by feelings of shame, disgust, and guilt.[7]

Anorexia: The Symptoms

The most noticeable physical symptom of anorexia is weight loss or, in children and teenagers who are still growing, the absence of normal weight gain. Clinically, patients are considered anorexic if their weight is 15 percent below the weight recommended for their height and age.

Over time people with anorexia show other apparent symptoms. These include brittle hair and nails, loss of hair, and dry, flaky skin that bruises easily. The palms of the hands and the soles of the feet become yellowish. Since anorexics' bodies are easily chilled, their skin grows fine hair (lanugo) to keep them warm.

More damaging changes happen inside the body of people with severe anorexia. They may become anemic and develop problems with their blood, as well as with their hearts, kidneys, digestive systems, muscles, joints, and bones. Women may experience an irregular menstrual period—or a stoppage of menstruation altogether (amenorrhea).

Anorexia also affects the brain in that victims have unrealistic perceptions not only about their body size but also about their relationships with others. They are likely to have disturbing emotional ups and downs. These may result in depression, insomnia, irritability, moodiness, and self-loathing.

The Mayo Clinic lists a number of "red flags" that warn that a person may have anorexia. They include:

- Skipping meals
- Making excuses for not eating
- Eating only a few "safe foods," usually those low in fat and calories
- Adopting rigid meal or eating rituals, such as cutting food into tiny pieces
- Spitting food out after chewing
- Weighing food
- Cooking elaborate meals for others but refusing to eat
- Repeated weighing of themselves
- Frequent checking in the mirror for perceived flaws
- Wearing baggy or layered clothing
- Complaining about being fat[8]

Anorexic Behavior

People with anorexia are obsessed with food. They typically try to lose weight by severely limiting the amount of food they eat. They may skip meals and lie about having eaten. When they eat with others, they may move food around on their plates without eating it. Or they may hide some of it in their napkins to dispose of later. They may take a very long time to eat very little. For example, one person with anorexia described taking an hour to eat an apple—her entire meal. Another tells how she divided a cookie into thirty-two sections to eat over several days.

Another way people with anorexia lose weight is through excessive, compulsive exercise. The results can be severe. Girls who exercise too much may change their menstrual cycle or cause it to stop entirely. In *The Truth About Eating Disorders* Gerri Kramer says, "People who exercise compulsively may experience dehydration, broken bones, torn ligaments, joint problems, osteoporosis, and even heart and kidney failure. A healthy amount of exercise builds muscle, but too much actually destroys the muscle."[9]

Kathiann Kowalski (who writes for many teen magazines) tells the story of Brianna, who had anorexia. Not only did Brianna starve herself to lose weight, she added to her risk by using diet pills. She stopped getting her period regularly, felt

Anorexics often have a distorted view of themselves, thinking they look heavier than they really are.

weak and had dizzy spells, lost hair, and was cold all the time. But she kept on dieting. Even after she lost 30 pounds (13.6kg), she was not satisfied. She decided to try nonstop exercising for three days. She would just start walking and keep on going. Kowalski says, "Fifteen hours later, Brianna walked into a police station. Her feet ached, her sweat-pants were covered with burrs from wandering through a park. She was exhausted, scared, and hungry. . . . Her grand exercise plan failed, but it had one good outcome. Brianna finally got help dealing with her problem."[10]

An Anorexic in the Making

Fifteen-year-old Gary was an outstanding baseball player for his high school team. Everyone, including his father and the professional scouts who came to watch him, expected him to

A Racial Bias?

Black anorexics may be more common than statistics show, according to reporter Shannah Tharp-Taylor, who says:

> Black women often suffer needlessly from anorexia because doctors do not expect to find eating disorders in the African American community and thus misdiagnose their anorexic patients. It has been thought that the African American community's greater acceptance of larger body sizes for women offers black teens some protection against anorexia. However, as African Americans take on the cultural values of the mainstream—white—culture, any protection provided by greater acceptance of diverse body types has diminished. While more research on eating disorders in minorities is needed, it appears that anorexia depends more on socioeconomic status than on race.

Shannah Tharp-Taylor, "Anorexia Among Black Women Gets New Scrutiny," *Chicago Tribune*, August 25, 2003, p. 1.

become a star pro player. Although he really did not want to play at such a highly competitive level, Gary felt pressured to live up to the expectations others had for him.

He began to train compulsively. Every morning he exercised two hours before school. He felt he had to do a hundred sit-ups at a time. After school he exercised with the baseball team. After dinner he exercised alone for another two hours.

He began to diet by cutting down on fatty foods and desserts. As he became obsessed with weight and calories he ate less and less food of any kind. He was 5 feet 7 inches (170 cm) tall, but even when his weight dropped to 104 pounds (47.3kg) he was not satisfied. He wanted to get down to 95 pounds (43.2kg). Gary says, "Over time it [the eating disorder] took over my entire life."[11]

Gary became extremely malnourished. When he had no body fat left to burn, his body began to burn muscle tissue. Very low blood pressure caused him to pass out frequently. He had to drop out of baseball and repeat his senior year in high school. For the next seven years he was in and out of the hospital with various ailments related to his anorexic behavior. He acknowledges now that anorexia almost ended his life.

Bulimia: The Symptoms

The signs of bulimia are often not as apparent as those of anorexia. People with bulimia may be of normal weight or slightly overweight. It is not obvious from looking at them that they are obsessed with their body weight and shape. Bulimics typically eat large amounts of food. This might be a whole cake instead of a slice, or a box of cookies instead of a few. Then, filled with horror of gaining weight, they engage in vomiting or misuse laxatives, diuretics, or enemas to purge the food from their bodies. Because their behavior takes place in secret, bulimics are often able to hide their disease for years.

Sometimes it is a dentist who first notices some of the telltale signs of bulimia. These include damaged teeth and gums. When a person vomits frequently, stomach acid wears away the enamel of his or her teeth and causes the teeth to turn brown. Frequent vomiting also causes sores in the throat and mouth. It may cause swelling of the salivary glands in the cheeks (commonly called "chipmunk cheeks"). And the chronic bulimic may become hoarse. Another clue to bulimic behavior is the appearance of bruises, sores, or calluses on the knuckles or fingers. These occur when the person gags him- or herself in order to vomit, and the fingers scrape against the teeth.

Internal damage caused by bulimia is more dangerous. With frequent vomiting, stomach acid burns the skin of the esophagus (the tube connecting the throat to the stomach). If the esophagus tears and bleeds it can be extremely painful. The frequent vomiting can also tear the stomach lining—a very serious development.

Bulimics typically eat large amounts of food—a whole cake instead of a slice, or a box of cookies instead of a few.

Frequent purging causes a chemical imbalance that may damage the kidneys. It may also cause an irregular heartbeat. Menstrual irregularities or amenorrhea may also occur. Excessive use of laxatives and diuretics may result in abnormal bowel functioning and dehydration.

Warning Signs of Bulimia

The Mayo Clinic has issued a list of emotional and behavioral symptoms associated with bulimia:

- Feeling that you can't control your eating behavior
- Eating until the point of discomfort or pain
- Eating much more food in a binge episode than in a normal meal or snack
- Exercising for hours on end
- Misuse of laxatives, diuretics or enemas
- Being preoccupied with your body shape and weight
- Having a distorted, excessively negative body image
- Going to the bathroom after eating or during meals
- Hoarding food
- Depression
- Anxiety[12]

Bulimic Behavior

Famous entertainer Elton John, who battled bulimia for fourteen years, describes what his life was like on a daily basis before he overcame the disease: "I would gorge myself then deliberately make myself sick. For breakfast I'd have an enormous fry-up, followed by 20 pots of cockles [shellfish] and then a tub of Haagen-Dazs vanilla. If I was eating a curry, I couldn't wait to throw it up so that I could have the next one."[13]

In *The Truth About Eating Disorders* an anonymous teenager describes his struggle with bulimia. He says at first his purging routines gave him a sense of power. He started each day by skipping breakfast. Since his mother worried about that, he would grab something to take with him. He did not want to waste the food, so he gave it to one of his hungry friends.

At lunch he ate something light, like a salad. But he worried that even that small amount of food would make him fat. So he

Elton John battled bulimia for fourteen years.

headed right from the cafeteria to a bathroom. When he first started purging he would stick his fingers down his throat. But it was not long before he could just think about vomiting and throw up.

At home after school he would scarf down chips, bread, sweets, and leftovers, carefully hiding the evidence. Sometimes he volunteered to do the grocery shopping so he could hide food in his room. After bingeing he would go upstairs and vomit. He not only felt relieved but also empowered. Then he exercised, did homework, exercised again. He even put folded-up blankets on the floor so he could run in place in his room late at night without anyone hearing him.

He began to make excuses to avoid school trips and parties and family shopping trips and gatherings. He knew the bathrooms would be too crowded for him to vomit in private. "One day," he says, "after lying in order to stay in the safety of my own home, I began to realize the purging was actually controlling me. Yet I wasn't sure I could stop. Finally, I did the hardest thing I've ever had to do. I asked for help."[14]

Crossover Eating Disorders

According to the testimony of many medical experts, incidences of anorexia and bulimia are frequently interlinked. A patient with bulimia often has a history of anorexia. When the anorexia is supposedly cured, the eating disorder reemerges as bulimia. According to one report, "During the course of the illness, individuals may receive several diagnoses, potentially meeting the criteria for anorexia, bulimia, and even binge-eating disorder (bulimia without compensatory acts after bingeing)."[15]

Liu's experience exemplifies how a person can progress from one eating disorder to another and back again. After her parents gave her the scale and diet books she had requested for Christmas, she began a serious study of dieting. Every

Jane Fonda Speaks Out

Award-winning actress Jane Fonda was one of the first Hollywood actresses to talk openly about eating disorders. Several years ago she revealed that she has struggled with anorexia and bulimia for thirty years—since she was twelve years old. In her memoir *My Life So Far* (Random House 2005), she talks about her dysfunctional childhood and her efforts to be perfect in whatever she did. Her anorexia and bulimia lasted through most of her acting career and continued through the years she was a fitness guru. After years of therapy and a religious conversion to Christianity, she came to accept that only God is perfect.

Today, Fonda shares what she has learned with therapists who treat eating disorders and with groups of patients suffering from anorexia and bulimia.

morning she weighed in. She bought a notebook and entered her daily intake down to the mouthful. She had five calorie counters, and if she could not find a food's calorie count in one of them, she stopped eating it.

She tried different fad diets. One of her schemes was the yogurt lunch. Mixing plain yogurt with fresh or water-packed fruits, she invented her own dietetic variations. It took her nearly half an hour to eat a cup of yogurt while her classmates were downing platefuls of spaghetti and salad, chocolate cake, and milk. Licking her spoon after each minuscule bite, she insisted she felt full. Her classmates were in awe of her self-discipline. Basking in her new fame, she did not dare let up for a minute.

She walked the two miles home from school whenever possible and spent every spare moment doing calisthenics. She tried to keep her body moving constantly. Her jumping jack routine became automatic until her mother demanded she stand still while they were talking. Each night, no matter how tired she was, she forced herself through an hour of strenuous shape-up exercises.

When her weight dropped from 130 pounds (59.1kg) to 105 pounds (47.7kg) she was ecstatic. Her success energized her, and she ignored the negatives involved. In fact, she was even pleased when her periods stopped. She was nearly always cold, bruised easily, and cuts and sores took months to heal. But she considered these necessary sacrifices.

Eventually her behavior swung back and forth between anorexia and bulimia. She never felt hungry, but she had a constant urge to gorge. Sometimes she would give in to it and eat a whole pan of fudge or an entire box of gingersnaps. She describes one night when she was babysitting (after dinner) and ate three jelly doughnuts, thirty-three butterscotch cookies, four three-inch squares of applesauce cake, five frozen sweet rolls, six slices of raisin bread, eight hunks of Muenster cheese, and a quarter of a roll of slice-and-bake cookie dough.

"It took me an hour to plough through all that," says Liu. "Then I spent the next three throwing up in the bathroom. When I got home I swallowed five tablets of Ex-Lax and spent most of the night and the next morning in the bathroom." She

Some anorexics engage in excessive exercising as a means of burning calories.

knew her behavior was "insane, appalling, reprehensible,"[16] but she could not stop herself.

Liu's struggle to regain normal eating patterns was long and painful. Then when her marriage seemed to be breaking up, she reverted to anorexic behavior. In *Gaining* she says, "With no one around for dinner, there was no one to notice that I skipped it—or that I weighed myself incessantly, or that I would go out for a walk and not return for hours. Only I knew what I was doing."[17]

Clearly it is difficult even to label eating disorder patients as having one disease or the other, since they may have a combination of diseases. And it is impossible to obtain an accurate count of the number of eating disorder victims at any given time, since many are so secretive about their problems with food. Despite these obstacles, intensive research is being done to uncover the causes of eating disorders and to discover effective ways of treating and preventing these potentially deadly diseases. In the meantime they continue to claim the lives of many victims.

CHAPTER TWO

Deadly Consequences of Anorexia and Bulimia

Medical experts estimate that when the number of suicides is added to the number of anorexic and bulimic patients who die from complications caused by their diseases, total fatalities amount to between 10 and 25 percent. Some people who have eating disorders refuse to believe their irrational behavior can have serious effects and do not seek help until it is too late to save their lives. Others feel their lives are worthless and that they do not deserve help. Often people with eating disorders become so addicted to their obsessive-compulsive behavior they resist any effort to change it. Others succeed in hiding their symptoms for long periods of time—sometimes many years—and delay efforts at recovery until it is impossible.

The Karen Carpenter Story

A shocking event can open the eyes of the world to a hidden danger. This happened when Karen Anne Carpenter died from anorexia in 1983 at the age of thirty-two. Although lots of people suffered from anorexia then, before her death the name of the disease was not widely known.

Karen was a musical sensation. She won national fame as a drummer before she became an enormously popular singer.

Self-Injury

For a person with an eating disorder, sometimes self-injury becomes a way of expressing the underlying pain that the patient cannot express in words. Self-harm may take the form of cutting, burning, branding with a hot object, hitting with an object such as a hammer, or banging some part of the body against a wall or floor. This kind of behavior came to public attention when Princess Diana of Britain admitted to having bulimia for a number of years. "That's like a secret disease," she said in an interview. "You inflict it upon yourself because your self-esteem is at a low ebb, and you don't think you're worthy or valuable. You fill your stomach up four or five times a day—some do it more—and it gives you a feeling of comfort. It's like having a pair of arms around you, but it's temporarily, temporary." During the unhappy years of her marriage to the heir to the British throne, Diana also admitted that she intentionally cut her arms and legs and had thrown herself down a flight of stairs on more than one occasion.

Quoted in www.edreferral.com/Celebrities_who_died_or_who_have_Eating_Disorders.htm.

She had perfect pitch and impeccable phrasing. She won three Grammys, eight gold albums, ten gold singles, and five platinum albums. She was on the front cover of national magazines and toured the world to win international fame.

Karen was attractive with a winning smile; large, dark eyes; and long, dark hair. But she hated that her body was a little on the plump side. When she reached 140 pounds (63.6kg), she began dieting obsessively and developed anorexia. In order to speed up her metabolism, she took ten times the normal daily dose of thyroid replacement medication (although her thyroid was normal). Combined with heavy doses of laxatives, this further weakened her heart and digestive system. When her weight dropped to 80 pounds (36.4kg), she began having serious health problems. After she collapsed on stage during a performance, she sought medical help.

Karen Carpenter (right) receives a Billboard Music Award in 1977. Six years later, she suffered cardiac arrest and died because of the toll anorexia had taken on her body.

She underwent treatment and believed she was recovering. She was planning to go public about her struggle with anorexia. But less than a month before her thirty-third birthday, Karen suffered cardiac arrest and died. The Los Angeles coroner gave the cause of her death as "heartbeat irregularities brought on by chemical imbalances associated with anorexia nervosa."[18]

Her death brought immediate and lasting media attention to anorexia and also to bulimia. A number of celebrities went public about their eating disorders. Calls and visits from people with eating disorders flooded medical centers and hospitals. Before the publicity about Karen's death, many of the victims had not known their disease had a name. Karen's family established the Karen A. Carpenter Memorial Foundation to raise money for research on anorexia and other eating disorders.

Christy Henrich: Dying for a Medal

Christy Henrich was a world-class American gymnast. She made the U.S. national gymnastics team, and in 1988 placed ninth at the Olympic Trials. In 1989 she won the silver medal in the all-around U.S. National Championships. She represented the United States at the World Championships in Stuttgart, Germany, placing fourth with the American team. One balance beam leap that she originated was named after her, and it is still included in the *Code of Points* for artistic gymnastics.

When a judge at the international meet in Stuttgart told Christy she needed to lose weight, she took the comment to heart. A five-year battle with her body began. She developed full-blown anorexia. Her 4-foot 11-inch frame (150cm) shrank from 90 pounds (40.9kg) to 47 pounds (21.4kg). Her alarmed family forced her to enter a hospital. She went through periods of recovery, relapses, and numerous treatments. But it was too late. The damage done to her body was too severe. Eight days after her twenty-second birthday, Christy died of multiple organ failure.

Her death caused a spotlight to be turned on the problem of eating disorders in gymnasts. Kim Arnold, a U.S. team member in the 1990s, said, "There was a lot of eating and purging. You used to see how little you can eat today and still get through a workout. We used to see how many meals we could miss before we had to eat again."[19]

According to Ron Thompson, codirector of an eating disorder program at Indiana's Bloomington Hospital, the gymnasts' youth and their driven personalities plus the competitive environment puts them at high risk for eating disorders. "These kids are so mentally tough, so willing to do anything the coach says will make them a better athlete," says Thompson. "They're perfectionists so continuing to train on broken bones and having eating disorders is normal behavior to them."[20]

Deadly Size Zero

Brazilian model Ana Carolina Reston dreamed of becoming a cover girl. In November 2006 her dream came true for all the wrong reasons. She was dead at the age of twenty-one from complications due to anorexia and bulimia. The world of fashion runway models was in an uproar, and she received more publicity than she could have ever dreamed of having.

Reston was the second South American model to die that year. Three months earlier, twenty-two-year-old Luisel Ramos of Uruguay had collapsed as she left the runway at a fashion show. She was rushed to a hospital where she died. Her death was attributed to heart failure caused by anorexia. For three months before her death she had reportedly lived on a diet of lettuce leaves and Diet Coke. On February 13, 2007, eighteen-year-old Eliana Ramos, Luisel's sister, died at their grandparents' home in Montevideo. Her death was caused by a heart attack that was blamed on malnutrition, leading to the assumption that she, too, was anorexic.

The body mass index (BMI) is a scale that uses a person's height and weight to determine the amount of body fat. The World Health Organization (WHO) considers a BMI of around sixteen to be starvation. At the time of her death, Luisel Ramos weighed about 98 pounds (44.5kg) despite being 5 feet 9 inches tall (175 cm). And her BMI was about 14.5—well below the starvation level. Luisel had literally starved herself to death.

The tragic fate of these young women shocked other celebrities into revealing their struggles with eating disorders. After

Luisel Ramos (left) and sister Eliana (right) were Uruguayan models who died within a year of each other at ages twenty-two and eighteen, respectively. Both suffered heart failure from anorexia.

years of denial, they now admit they have suffered from eating disorder obsessions that have come close to destroying their lives. Realizing how close to death they themselves have come, they now speak out to warn others about the possible fatal effects of trying to be size zero.

The Barbi Twins

In the mid 1990s identical twin sisters Shane and Sia Barbi appeared on the covers of two of *Playboy*'s top-selling issues. They became famous as the "Barbi Twins" and started a multimillion-dollar calendar business (featuring pictures of themselves). Movie and TV scripts were written exclusively for them. And they became heroines in a series of comic books featuring stories about them. At the peak of their careers, they dropped out of their hectic schedule to recover from their life-and-death struggle with bulimia.

They talked to reporters about their quest to be pinup perfect for every photo opportunity. Sia says, "I went feast and famine, feast and famine. That was my whole life. There was no such thing as sitting down to a normal meal. I did ten hours of exercise seven days a week. I was in so much pain all the time."[21] Eventually the sisters became full-blown bulimics. Sia took laxatives and Shane vomited. At one point the 5-foot 9-inch sisters (175cm) each weighed just over 100 pounds (45.5kg). When Sia collapsed after taking more than one hundred laxatives, her doctor warned her that she would die if she did not stop her obsessive behavior.

Since then the Barbi twins have recovered from their eating disorders. And they have made a study of the disease that almost killed them. They have become activists in the fight against eating disorders. They have written a book, *Dying to Be Healthy*. And they tour high schools and colleges, warning young women not to make the same mistakes they did.

Mary-Kate Olsen

Mary-Kate's career began at the age of nine months when she and her twin, Ashley, were hired to play the same character in the television series *Full House*. Child labor laws limited how many hours they could work, so the sisters took turns during the tapings. The series had an eight-year run, during which the twins gained an eager fan club of young girls.

When *Full House* ended, the Olsen sisters used their fame to establish a company called Dualstar and began marketing their image. They have had huge success with the preteen market. They have their own line of videos, books, dolls, video games, fragrances, and a Wal-Mart clothing label. They also have continued their lucrative acting careers. At the age of eighteen they took over control from the trustees who were managing their empire worth an estimated $300 million.

Success, fame, and wealth, however, did not ensure happiness or health. A little more than a week after her eighteenth

Although she denied having an eating disorder, Mary-Kate Olsen (left) became noticeably thinner than her twin, Ashley (right). Her family staged an intervention and sent her to rehab.

birthday, Mary-Kate checked into a rehab center for six weeks to be treated for anorexia nervosa. For years she had denied she had an eating disorder, despite the concern of family and friends. When she became noticeably thinner than her twin and developed dark circles under her eyes, her fans also began expressing anxiety about her health. Still, Mary-Kate continued in denial until an intervention by her family sent her into rehab.

Her recovery was not easy. Speaking about the long struggle, she admits that at times she just wanted to give up the fight. "There have definitely been times in my life," she says, "when I just turned to people and said, 'I'm done—this is too much for me. This is too overwhelming.'"[22]

The Road to Suicide

In 2008 the results of a study conducted at the University of Vermont were published. They reported that people with anorexia also have a significantly increased risk of suicide. The report said: "Anorexia has the highest mortality rate of any psychiatric disorder. But psychologists previously believed that those high rates of death were due to patients' already deteriorated physical state. . . . The new study's authors have shown this assumption to be wrong in most cases."[23] The researchers emphasized the need to treat anorexia both physically and psychologically. The extreme methods used in the suicide attempts led the researchers to conclude that the patients were genuinely determined to die.

Geri

Eating disorders specialist Marc Zimmer had a patient who nearly succeeded in killing herself. At first purging her body gave Geri a sense of control and made her feel good. She fasted, binged, purged, and felt "totally clean."

Talk therapy and biofeedback therapy seemed to put her on the road to recovery. Then a big blow-up in her family occurred. Geri felt useless and desperate. She says, "It was as if I had a total eclipse inside my head, and a giant painful mass blocked out every bit of life I had in me. I just went into the bathroom, locked the door, smashed the mirror on the medicine cabinet, took a piece of glass, and hacked at my wrists until I passed out." Fortunately she survived that crisis and returned to therapy. "Living meant changing," she says, "and I know I'm here today because I chose life."

Ira M. Sacker and Marc A Zimmer, *Dying to Be Thin*. New York: Warner, 1987, pp. 159–61.

Scott Crow, University of Minnesota psychiatrist and eating disorder specialist, says, "Eating disorders have the second highest death rates of any mental illness (only opium addicts have a higher one), and the highest suicide rates."[24] During a ten-year study of anorexics, Crow found that 10 percent had died of their disease, either from medical complications like heart failure or from suicide.

Sherri came very close to dying from anorexia. Her eating disorder began when she was eight, but it was not until thirty years later that she was diagnosed with anorexia nervosa. In the May 5, 2008, issue of *American Medical News*, correspondent Kathleen Tomaselli described Sherri's pattern of behavior:

> It was a daily menu of gum and tea sprinkled with 20 or so over-the-counter diet and water pills, 10 laxatives and six hours running on the treadmill. A few times a week, she would cut on her body with knives she kept taped under chairs, a release of pain, anger and starved emotions. At night she would lie awake, agonizing about how she could stay committed to this regimen.[25]

When Sherri finally sought help, her heart was beating so slowly she was told she would die in a month without treatment. She finally agreed to undergo treatment when she became convinced that she was on the road to suicide. Unfortunately, some people with anorexia and bulimia persist in staying on that road until the bitter end.

Michael Krasnow: Male Anorexic

Michael Krasnow had a normal childhood with loving, supportive parents. His mother was president of the PTA and volunteered at the school library. His father coached the Little League baseball team. They never missed a single event in which Michael or his brother participated.

Michael's life changed when he began high school. He felt depressed and began showing signs of obsessive-compulsive behavior. First it was studying. He began by studying from the time he got home from school until midnight. Then he studied until 1:00 A.M.—then until 2:00. Eventually, he went to bed at 2:00 and

His obsessive-compulsive behavior of brushing his teeth up to twelve times a day led one male anorexic to avoid eating to keep his mouth clean.

set his alarm for 4:00 so he could study some more before leaving for school. He even studied on the bus ride to school. Every piece of homework had to be perfect without one erasure mark, no matter how many times he had to copy it over.

When his parents could not convince him he was damaging his health, they sent him to a psychiatrist. It was decided he should withdraw from school. This did stop the compulsive studying, but Michael soon had another obsession—tooth brushing. He began by brushing his teeth two hours a day. Soon it was twelve hours a day. He would brush while walking around or sitting in front of the television. After about two weeks he really hated the tooth brushing. And he reasoned that if he did not eat anything, his mouth would be clean, and he would not have to brush.

He began to severely limit his food intake. In his autobiography, *My Life as a Male Anorexic*, he describes his descent into anorexia. He tried to survive on seven hundred calories a day. He refused to let anyone see him eat. He quit drinking water because it made him feel fat. And he refused to swallow his own saliva. He did not want to swallow the calories it might contain. So he spit it out into a paper cup or a paper towel, which he carried in his pocket.

Michael's distressed parents tried sending him to different doctors who specialized in eating disorders. He was in and out of hospitals. As self-starvation became more addictive, he became rail thin. And he took pride in finding tricks to resist the plans to help him. He survived to the age of twenty-eight—just barely.

In the epilogue to his book he says, "Everything is basically the same. I'm still 75 pounds, still have 1,000 calories per day, still don't care if I live or die. In other words, I still exist, but nothing else; and as I've said all along, it's only a matter of time until I fast and starve myself to death."[26] Shortly after he wrote these words, Michael died alone, having deliberately starved himself to death.

In an article on anorexia and suicide, Matthew Tiemeyer points out that anorexia serves the purpose of relieving certain kinds of stress. "For some," he says, "it might be relationship or family problems. Others need to numb the pressure to perform. Regardless, an eating disorder *exchanges one kind of stress for another*. But if the stress of the eating disorder grows out of control, the person is trapped between two unbearable sources of anxiety. Suicide can seem like the only way out."[27]

In *The Secret Language of Eating Disorders*, psychologist Peggy Claude-Pierre says that the risk of suicide in patients with acute eating disorders is high because they are so weary of fighting. She quotes one young woman: "I'm 24 years old and have had an eating disorder for 8 years. I've been in and out of the hospital for this a dozen times. It's not that I don't want to get better, I do. It's just that I have tried so many things and it just seems hopeless. Suicide is looking better and better every day. I'm not sure what else to do."[28]

In order to prevent this kind of hopelessness and possible tragic ending, medical experts are working to discover the causes that underlie destructive eating patterns.

CHAPTER THREE

Causes of Anorexia and Bulimia

Experts agree that people develop eating disorders for many reasons. Some of the reasons are known, but many are not. People whose lives are unhappy may turn to food for comfort or use it as a way of feeling that they are in control of their lives. Before they are aware of what is happening, they may become obsessed with food and weight. Experts also agree that some of the deeper causes of eating disorders are only beginning to be understood. People who are stressed, lonely, or depressed sometimes develop unhealthy eating habits. They may gorge on food they love and harshly purge it from their bodies. Other people starve themselves thinking they will be more loveable or more popular if they are thinner. Still others become victims of eating disorders because of the competitive nature of their careers. Whatever their reason for trying to cope with life's difficulties through food, they are putting themselves in serious danger.

Control Through Perfectionism

Every perfectionist does not develop an eating disorder, but many people who develop eating disorders are perfectionists. Liu, who has studied eating disorders in depth, says that perfectionism is the most consistent trait among both anorexics and bulimics. "Most people who have had an eating disorder,"

Perfectionism is the most consistent trait among anorexics and bulimics. For example, receiving an A-minus on a book report can cause feelings of failure because it was not an A-plus.

she says, "believe down to their nerve endings that perfection is a real, attainable noble state and that it is their right and duty to claim it, whether they are performing in a play, organizing a closet, planning a party, or anticipating a date."[29] The trouble with perfection, she explains, is that it is unattainable. Every human fails from time to time. And every human makes mistakes. So perfectionists are in a constant state of frustration and disappointment.

One patient with an eating disorder wrote in her journal: "I cannot recognize or appreciate any of my own accomplishments. Others are always better. Even when I achieve excellence it isn't good enough. I recently got 98 percent on my calculus final and was upset with myself for not doing better. My goals are far too high. I lose sight of what is realistic or even excellent, and strive for what is impossible."[30]

Many eating disorder patients are overachievers. This was true of Michael Krasnow, who studied compulsively and refused to allow a single erasure on his homework. Even when his perfectionism frustrated him so much that he banged his head against the wall, he could not control it. In the end he believed the only thing in his life he could control was the amount of food he ate—or refused to eat.

Ira Sacker, a leader in the field of eating disorders, says that perfectionists put themselves in cages through their rigid behavior. They may become procrastinators, putting off important projects because they are afraid they cannot live up to their own high standards. Or they may be excessively active. As an example he tells about a patient named Brenda who was a college student. The minute a paper was assigned she began to work on it endlessly. She researched the subject from every possible angle. When she began the actual writing, she went through draft after draft. But she always thought she could do

A Tip from NEDA

The National Eating Disorders Association urges everyone to become a critic of information that appears in all forms of the media. NEDA says: "One of the ways we can protect our self-esteem and body image from the media's often narrow definitions of beauty and acceptability is to become a critical viewer of the media messages we are bombarded with each day."

www.nationaleatingdisorders.org/information-resources/general-information.php.

better. So despite the huge amount of work she put into every paper, she was always late in handing it in. Sacker says:

> Perfectionists will judge their body image by the more un-realistic standards set by the society around us. These demands for perfection are unrealistic and virtually impossible to achieve. They're formed not by the reality of what a healthy body should look like, but by the endless media images of so-called perfect bodies that bombard us every day. That sort of perfection isn't really something any normal person can attain without major body-altering means such as extremely strenuous exercise, starvation dieting, and cosmetic surgery, but the images are still very, very powerful. Combine our societal pressure to be slender with a perfectionist's drive to be perfect, and what you get is someone who will be very vulnerable to a major eating disorder.[31]

Body Image and Self-Esteem

In *It's Not About the Weight,* professor of psychology Susan Mendelsohn says that eating disorders are physical manifestations arising from internal causes. The driving force of the disease, she points out, is the fear, insecurity, and emotional turmoil that lie deep inside.

Concern with body image may begin at home with innocent remarks from parents who warn against eating too much and becoming fat. Other relatives such as Liu's grandmother who called her "chubby" can add to the concern. Siblings and classmates are apt to think up even more hurtful nicknames. And as Mendelsohn says:

> Home and school are not the only breeding grounds for body image derailment. What

about the candy store clerk who "cuts you off" after a few candy bars, the local hoods who shout insults from their car windows as they pass, or the beloved neighbor who has a nickname for everyone, usually to reflect the opposite of how they appear. The town giant is "Tiny," the city octogenarian is "Youngun," and you're "Slim," nicknamed with a know-it-all grin.[32]

One study showed that some teenage girls have negative feelings about their bodies after watching ultrathin models on television.

Unfortunately the importance American society places on physical beauty and thinness helps undermine the self-esteem of vulnerable children. Size 00 models and celebrities are constantly splashed across the media. Heroes and heroines are usually beautiful and slim. Characters with plump bodies may be supportive best friends, but they are not the stars.

A study made in 2002 examined how teenagers felt after watching soap operas and other TV shows, reading magazines, and watching music videos that emphasized the thin ideal. The researchers concluded that most of the teens had negative feelings about their own bodies after seeing the unrealistic models.

Other studies have documented the powerful influence of TV. Anne Becker, a professor at Harvard Medical School, published a study describing what happened in Fiji, a small island nation in the Pacific Ocean, before and after television arrived. Before American television arrived, Fijians considered the ideal body to be plump, round, and soft. After three years of watching shows like *Melrose Place* and *Beverly Hills 90210*, teenage girls showed serious signs of eating disorders. The Harvard study found that Fijian teens who watched three or more nights of TV per week were apt to consider themselves too fat. They told investigators they had begun dieting and vomiting to control their weight.

Deadly Web Sites

Although much blame has been directed at the fashion and entertainment media for promoting behavior that leads to eating disorders, the influence of peer-driven Web sites may be even more dangerous. Pro ana (pro anorexia) and pro mia (pro bulimia) Web sites have grown into the hundreds in the last few years in several countries. The sites are usually generated by girls suffering from anorexia or bulimia who have permissive attitudes toward these illnesses.

Usually the sites claim they have no interest in recruiting girls who are not already victims of eating disorders, but experts refute this claim. Psychotherapist Steven Levenkron says: "The girls who run these sites are lonely, and instead of calling themselves sick, they get to feel like they have a career.

. . . Many of them have no social life, and their only hope is to find other anorexics. But it's negative energy coalescing: It seduces girls into anorexia, and makes the girl who runs it feel less lonely."[33]

France was the first country to recognize that these sites encourage susceptible young women to develop eating disorders and the first to pass laws banning them. Pro ana and pro mia sites in the United States post images of emaciated women as "thinspiration," inspiring their watchers to adopt dangerous eating habits.

"Catching" an Eating Disorder

Eating disorders are not contagious in the same way as measles or the flu, but the *idea* of having an eating disorder can be catching. The *Urban Dictionary* defines "wannarexic" as "someone who wishes or pretends they have an eating disorder or deliberately goes out of their way to make it look like they have anorexia."[34] Encouraged by Web sites and/or groups that promote unrealistic thinness, the wannarexic can easily acquire a real eating disorder.

Sometimes anorexia can spread throughout a group. In *Going Hungry* Kate Taylor says: "A friend of mine who attended an elite girls' school in Manhattan says the widespread view of parents, teachers, and students at her school was that anorexia was a contagious illness, spread by one alpha dieter to her impressionable friends. 'There was a group of girls, led by J., who would eat broccoli and mustard for lunch,' my friend remembers."[35] Eventually, Taylor reports, J. was hospitalized with severe anorexia.

At least three members of the popular British musical group the Spice Girls have admitted to suffering from eating disorders. Geri Halliwell says she developed eating disorders while living with the other Spice Girls. She felt she was fat compared to other band members and developed bulimia trying to lose weight. The fact that she was called "Podge Spice" added to her bad self-image. Victoria Beckham (Posh Spice) says that Geri encouraged her and Melanie Chisholm (Sporty Spice) to take up running and to eat liquid meals. Eventually Victoria started to binge eat and once ate ten bowls of cereal at a sitting.

Melanie starved herself and exercised excessively. She says:

> It's easy to be influenced by another person's behavior
> when you spend lots of time with them. And once you
> start losing weight, it's very addictive. . . . My diet became
> more and more restrictive, until I was just eating fruit and
> veg. I went on faddy diets and didn't touch protein or car-
> bohydrates, which was ridiculous, as we were running
> around like maniacs. I was under weight and living on
> adrenalin.[36]

At least three members of the British music group the Spice Girls
admitted to suffering from an eating disorder. Geri Halliwell (left) said
that she felt "fat" compared to the other members of the group.

The Pressure of Performing

Successful athletes are under heavy pressure. They set high goals for themselves. They are usually more determined and more disciplined than the average individual. The competitive sports environment adds to the pressure. Anxiety about their performances and negative self-appraisal can lead to excessive concern about their physiques and to eating disorders.

Although eating disorders are found in all sports, people in activities that emphasize leanness for performance and appearance are at much greater risk. Wrestlers and jockeys who have to meet rigid weight requirements may develop unhealthy ways of losing or gaining weight. Swimming, diving, dancing, track, and gymnastics require strong, light bodies.

In an article written for Vanderbilt University, Ana Cintado explains one reason gymnasts are vulnerable to eating disorders:

> Anorexia often strikes young women who try to evade the natural process of becoming adults and who use excessive measures to maintain a thin and girlish figure—the exact description of what today's female gymnast must accomplish to stay competitive at the highest levels. For these athletes, the onset of womanhood is their biggest fear because it means developing hips or breasts that might hinder their performance. Thus, starving themselves offers the most convenient solution to their problem.[37]

Cintado also blames authoritarian coaches who try to shame the girls into losing weight or even punish team members who exceed their assigned weight. And she mentions the judging system as sharing responsibility for the gymnasts' dissatisfaction with their bodies and their drive for thinness. She cites the incident of a U.S. judge telling Christy Henrich she would have to lose weight to make the Olympic team. Christy thought she was fat, she told her mother, and she began a strenuous effort to lose weight. Christy succeeded but in the process developed anorexia and bulimia and died of multiple organ failure.

Performers with eating disorders may wreck their careers. This almost happened to Katharine McPhee, *American Idol* finalist in

"Oink Olympics"

Journalist Scott M. Reid has investigated the heavy emphasis on thinness for gymnasts. Weight consciousness, he says, is drilled into gymnasts as young as five, who are weighed every day. Older gymnasts are sometimes weighed twice a day. Her coach called Patti Massoels, a national team member, a "pig." At the time, Patti says she weighed 90 pounds (40.9kg) and was living on two graham crackers a day. Reid says: "Gymnasts not making prescribed weights receive punishments ranging from the withholding of food to being required to do extra workouts. It is not uncommon for penalized gymnasts to work out in saunas wearing rubber suits. At one gym the practice is referred to as the "Oink Olympics."

Quoted in www.gymmedia.com/FORUM/agforum/05_01_henrich_e.htm.

Eating disorders are prevalent in the world of gymnastics. Female gymnasts are pressured to maintain very lean bodies to maintain their competitive edge.

2006. She had struggled with bulimia for five years. At the worst times, she was vomiting as many as seven times a day. Her vocal cords could have been ruined. But when she made it through her audition, she decided to seek help. McPhee says:

> I knew I had put off going to a treatment center long enough. I'd been struggling with bulimia since I was 17. Growing up in Los Angeles and spending all those years in dance class, I'd been conscious of body image at a young age, and I went through phases of exercising compulsively and starving myself. . . . Food was my crutch; it was how I dealt with emotions and uncomfortable situations.[38]

The Genetic Factor

Many researchers are studying genetic factors to learn how they may contribute to developing eating disorders. A study published in March 2002 in the *American Journal of Psychiatry* found that relatives of women with anorexia were eleven times more likely to have anorexia, and relatives of women with bulimia had an almost four times greater risk for bulimia than women who had no family history of eating disorders.

Sacker says that when he first began treating patients with eating disorders, he did not pay much attention to the eating patterns of their parents. He was surprised to discover that many parents admitted they too had experienced some kind of disordered eating in their past. He now believes eating disorders have a genetic component. Sacker says: "Having a family history of eating disorder, addictions, and obsessive-compulsive behavior doesn't guarantee that someone will develop an eating disorder. It does suggest, however, that awareness of the possibility needs to be present, just as there needs to be an awareness of a family history of, say, breast cancer or diabetes."[39]

A study at Medical College of Virginia at Virginia Commonwealth University focused on identical and fraternal twins. The researchers found that pairs of identical twins had a much higher incidence of eating disorders than fraternal twins did. Because identical twins have the same genes, the scientists concluded that heredity plays a role in eating disorders. They

Because of their genetic makeup, identical twins have a higher incidence of eating disorders than fraternal twins.

also pointed out that environmental and emotional factors might make twins particularly susceptible. For instance, the fact that twins are constantly being compared with each other and judged as being bigger, taller, thinner, or heavier may distort their body image.

The Chemical Connection

Many studies show that people with anorexia or bulimia are often clinically depressed, but which comes first is still uncertain. Does the depression lead to the eating disorder, or does the eating disorder cause the depression? Or do the two coincide? These questions are being studied by various groups of experts.

The chemical compound serotonin appears in many reports from these studies. Fairburn has done extensive research in eating disorders. He says:

> Interestingly, dieting has been shown to affect certain chemical transmitters in the brain, particularly serotonin, and this effect is more pronounced in women than in men. Since serotonin is thought to play a role in the normal control of eating as well as in food selection, this finding is intriguing. . . . Put simply, it seems that an abnormality in brain serotonin function may put people at risk of developing bulimia nervosa and that dieting in women may exaggerate this risk.[40]

Professor of health education Mark Kittleson points out that serotonin is one of the neurotransmitters that give a person a sense of physical and emotional fulfillment. He says, "Serotonin, in particular, sends the message that you feel full and have had enough to eat. Researchers have found that acutely ill patients suffering from anorexia and bulimia have significantly lower levels of serotonin."[41]

In 2004 researchers at the National Institute of Mental Health (NIMH) identified a rare gene mutation found in people with anorexia nervosa. This mutation creates an imbalance in serotonin. And NIMH says it may help to explain why eating disorders and depression so frequently overlap.

Hormones are also being studied in connection with eating disorders. These chemicals originate in the glands and are carried throughout the body by the blood. It has been discovered that people with eating disorders tend to have high levels of the hormones vasopressin and cortisol. Both of these hormones are released in response to stress. Another hormone, cholecystokinin (CCK), has been shown to make laboratory animals feel so full they stop eating. Tests show that people with bulimia tend to have low CCK levels.

The Tangled Roots of Eating Disorders

The *Harvard Mental Health Letter* of February 2003 mentions the possibility of an anorexic personality. "Girls and women with the disorder are often shy, neat, quiet, conscientious, and hypersensitive to rejection. They are prey to irrational guilt, feelings of inferiority, and obsessive worrying. They have unrealistic hopes of perfection and feel as though they can never meet their own standards."[42]

Sarah Haight is a fashion writer whose work has appeared in *Vogue, Teen Vogue, Women's Wear Daily*, and *W* magazine. In discussing the causes of her eating disorder she says,

> Anorexia is one of the most difficult illnesses to trace the origins of: Its roots are tangled, and the delicate unbinding of each contributing factor can be done only once the patient has truly agreed to get help. In my case, the disease was the product of a complicated mélange of emotional pain, perfectionism, societal pressure, and genetic bad luck. Every anorexic has a narrative of where things started to go awry.[43]

In *Anatomy of Anorexia* Levenkron explores the causes of anorexia and the reasons only a small minority of people who develop anorexia recover without help. His conclusions about anorexia can also apply to bulimia. Levenkron states: "Anorexia begins with a desire to be thin, a need to feel secure, to eliminate self-doubts and poor self-esteem, along with worries about the future."[44] As the disease progresses, he points out, it becomes more valuable to the personality, giving its victim a sense of control and identity. Such valuable support can be very hard to give up.

The past decade has seen a shift in research into the causes of eating disorders, away from explanations that rely solely on psychological or social factors to include the significance of genetic factors and chemical disturbances. The more the multiple factors underlying eating disorders are uncovered, the more complicated (and necessary) it is to develop treatment strategies that are effective.

CHAPTER FOUR

Treating Anorexia and Bulimia

Eating disorders can be difficult and frustrating for doctors and therapists to diagnose and treat. With most diseases, patients are eager to describe their symptoms and report every clue they can think of that might help diagnose and lead to a cure of their illnesses. Anorexics and bulimics, on the other hand, often go to great lengths to conceal their symptoms and frequently lie to their doctors or therapists about their eating habits. Despite the patient's secretiveness, however, definite signs, symptoms, and tests can be used to confirm that the patient has an eating disorder. But after the diagnosis, unfortunately, no one-size-fits-all treatment will cure the disease. Every patient with anorexia or bulimia has a unique history. Only after the underlying causes of the patient's disease are uncovered can the best treatment be designed to fit his or her particular needs. And recovery is often a very long process with many pitfalls.

Resisting Treatment

The first hurdle that must be cleared before treatment can begin for patients with addictive behaviors is for them to want to be cured. This is true for people addicted to alcohol, nicotine, and other drugs, as well as those addicted to harmful eating habits.

One of the biggest problems in treating anorexia and bulimia is that people who have these diseases often have a strong desire *not* to be cured. They have a love/hate relationship with their disease. They believe it empowers them by giving them a way to control their lives. They are terribly afraid of what will happen when this prop is removed. It is as hard for them to give up their obsessive behavior as it is for a confirmed cigarette smoker or a person addicted to alcohol to quit his or her habit.

One of the biggest challenges for anorexics and bulimics is to recognize that they have a problem and to seek medical help.

In her book *Wasted* Marya Hornbacher describes the way this addiction takes control of the victim's life:

> Eating disorders are addictions. You become addicted to a number of their effects. The two most basic and important: the pure adrenaline that kicks in when you're starving— you're high as a kite, sleepless, full of a frenetic unstable energy—and the heightened intensity of experience that eating disorders initially induce. At first, everything tastes and smells intense, tactile experience is intense, your own drive and energy themselves are intense and focused. Your sense of power is very, very intense. You are not aware, however, that you are quickly becoming addicted. And there's the rub. As with drugs, the longer you do it, the more you need to achieve that original high.[45]

No wonder many eating disorder survivors resist being deprived of this escape from the problems in their lives that are overwhelming them.

Filling the Void

Eating disorders expert Ira M. Sacker says truly letting go of an eating disorder means leaving a safe place. The job of the therapist, he says, is to help his or her patients find new, safer ways to handle anxiety and cope with life's changes and transitions. Everyone, he points out, has interests and passions. The challenge is to discover them. To someone with an eating disorder, trying something new may be upsetting or panic inducing. Sacker encourages his patients to stay in school or to return if they have dropped out. "Part of this is purely practical," he says. "In today's society, a college degree is essential for any sort of meaningful employment. The large reason, however, is that school is a place to find and pursue a passion that can become a career-driven pathway."

Ira M. Sacker, *Regaining Your Self*. New York: Hyperion, 2007, p. 147.

In *Dying to Be Thin* Sacker tells the story of Leslie to illustrate the difficulty of treating resistant patients. Leslie came very close to dying from bulimia. She denied she was sick and resisted treatment until she became so ill she had to be hospitalized. When she entered the hospital she was 5 feet 8 inches tall (173cm) and weighed 89 pounds (40.5kg). Sacker says that Leslie felt guilty and angry with herself for letting her sickness get so bad.

> She had agreed not to lose any more weight, and she knew that if she lost even one pound, she would be put into the hospital. And she kept on losing weight. One side of her knew she had forced the doctor and her parents to hospitalize her. But the other voice inside her kept saying, "You'll beat this. Just do what they want really fast and get out, because they'll make you fat and disgusting, after you've worked so hard to get this thin."[46]

Diagnosing Anorexia

The most obvious symptom of anorexia is extreme weight loss resulting in a skeletal appearance. The American Psychiatric Association's criteria for diagnosing anorexia are:

- Refusal to maintain a body weight that is at or above the minimum normal weight for your age and height
- Intense fear of gaining weight or becoming fat, even though you're underweight
- Denying the seriousness of having a low body weight, or having a distorted image of your appearance or shape
- In women who've started having periods, the absence of a period in at least three consecutive menstrual cycles[47]

Medical professionals agree these are important symptoms to check in diagnosing anorexia. In addition, doctors check for other signs, including hair that thins, breaks, or falls out; brittle nails; dry skin with a yellowish tinge; and soft, downy hair covering the body. The anorexic may suffer dizziness or fainting spells, fatigue, dehydration, constipation, low blood pressure, and an intolerance of cold. Behavioral and emotional symptoms include refusing to eat, excessive exercise, compulsive actions, difficulty concentrating, and a lack of emotion.

Treating Anorexia

Anorexia is a complicated disease that is not easy to treat. With patients who deny their illness and resist efforts at treatment, it becomes doubly difficult to cure. When anorexia leads to severe malnutrition or medical complications such as heart problems or psychiatric emergencies, hospitalization on a medical or psychiatric ward may be necessary.

Today many clinics specialize in eating disorder programs. Some of these are residential and admit patients for long periods of time. This kind of care is especially important for patients who need close monitoring. Other clinics offer daily outpatient programs. These programs are more likely to be successful for young patients whose families are supportive and involved in their treatment plans.

Many organizations and noted eating disorder specialists believe that both the physical and emotional problems underlying anorexia have to be treated. Treatment plans usually include treating any serious medical problems first, then focusing on weight gain to a safe level, and then exploring the psychological problems that led to the development of the disease. The Mayo Clinic offers this advice to victims of anorexia: "Individual, family and group therapy may all be beneficial. . . . In psychotherapy, you can gain a healthier self-esteem and learn positive ways to cope with distress and other strong feelings."[48]

Many factors have to be considered in working out the type of treatment that will be most likely to succeed with a particular patient. These include the person's age and his or her overall physical condition. Other considerations are how quickly the patient has been losing weight, the length of his or her illness, and information about previous treatments. Also important is how willing the patient is to cooperate in exploring the psychological problems underlying the disease.

In severe cases of malnutrition hospitalized patients may be hooked up to tubes so they can receive nutrients intravenously. This can be a life-saving measure when the patient is at the point

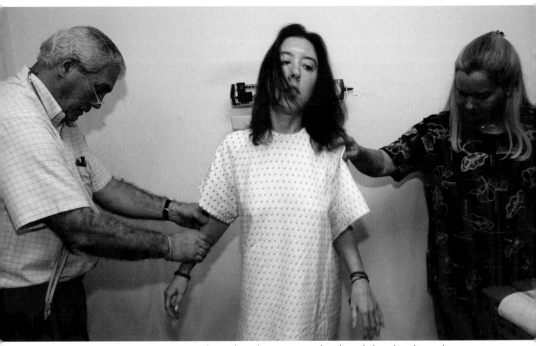

A woman at an eating disorder clinic is weighed with her back to the scale so she cannot see her weight gain. Some residential clinics admit patients who need close monitoring for long periods of time.

of dying from the effects of starvation. An advantage of treating patients in a hospital or residential clinic setting is that their food intake and their weight can be carefully watched and recorded. Inpatient treatment is important for patients who are seriously emaciated. And it is necessary for those who need close medical monitoring or are at serious risk for self-harm.

Diagnosing Bulimia

Since people with bulimia often have bodies that look normal, it is necessary to use signs other than weight to diagnose the disease. Some professionals categorize the disease in two ways. Purging bulimia occurs when the patient regularly engages in vomiting or the misuse of laxatives, diuretics, or enemas to compensate for binges. Exercise bulimia occurs when the patient overexercises with or without fasting. Excessive exercise then becomes the way of purging the body of calories.

Frequent vomiting leaves signs that alert the doctor to the possibility of bulimia. These include sores, scars, or calluses on the knuckles or hands, damaged teeth and gums, swollen salivary glands in the cheeks, and sores in the throat and mouth. The doctor will also check the patient for bloating, dehydration, dry skin, and an irregular heartbeat. He or she will ask about abnormal bowel functioning and menstrual irregularities. And the doctor will also check for signs that the patient has performed acts of self-harm such as cutting, burning, or hitting themselves.

Only when depression and anxiety make them seek professional help are some bulimics willing to admit to hoarding food; exercising for hours on end; misusing laxatives, diuretics, or enemas; eating to the point of pain; and the feeling that they cannot control their eating behavior. Until the patient is willing to cooperate, deeper emotional and behavioral symptoms of bulimia are harder to uncover. And curing the dedicated bulimic may be still harder.

Treating Bulimia

Like people with anorexia, most bulimics usually do not get better on their own. This is especially true if the disease has been going on for a long time. When bulimia is suspected, the doctor will perform a physical exam and order laboratory tests. These may include a complete blood count and specialized blood tests to check electrolytes and protein, as well as liver, kidney, and thyroid function.

The doctor or a mental health professional will ask patients about their eating habits. He or she will ask about bulimia symptoms and will try to learn how the patient feels about them, how severe they are, and how they affect the person's life. The patient may also be asked to fill out a questionnaire designed to uncover psychological problems.

Bulimic patients with serious health complications may need to be hospitalized until their condition can be stabilized. Complications that require hospitalization may include severe anemia, tearing of the stomach lining, damaged kidneys, or an irregular heartbeat.

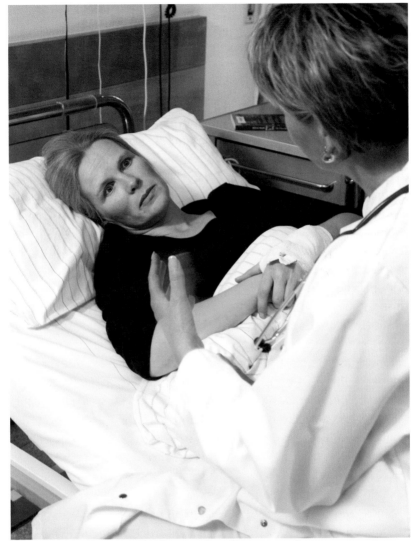

Some bulimics have to be hospitalized because of severe anemia, tearing of the stomach lining, damaged kidneys, or an irregular heartbeat.

A team approach is often used in treatment. The team includes a doctor or other medical provider, a mental health provider, and a dietitian. A case manager may be assigned to coordinate the patient's care. If the patient is well enough, he or she participates in making decisions about treatment options.

When necessary, specialized eating disorder clinics provide intensive treatment for weeks or months. Also available are clinics and programs that offer outpatient day treatment.

Recovery Through Self-Discovery

Sometimes a person with an eating disorder realizes he or she is on a path that is leading to self-destruction and pulls back in time. Just as some smokers can stop their risky behavior without professional help, these individuals recover on their own—or with the help of family and friends. Lana D'Amico was one of these.

Lana wanted to be a ballerina for as long as she could remember. She loved her ballet classes. When she was not in ballet class, she was not interested in going to the mall with her friends or in dating. She preferred to spend her time watching videos of ballet and daydreaming of performing on the stage. She believed she was not thin enough to be a ballerina although her coach did not encourage her to lose weight.

When she was accepted at the Richmond Ballet's Summer Dance Program, she moved to Virginia. Facing competition against talented dancers from all across the country, she pushed herself to improve her dancing and to lose weight. She danced from ten in the morning until six at night and ate only one meal a day.

Journaling

Eating disorder specialist Susan J. Mendelsohn urges her patients to keep a journal. It is not, she explains "a quick fix," but the cumulative effects can be "simply amazing." It is an outlet for venting and can be an alternate behavior for bingeing, purging, and other harmful behavior. At the very least, Mendelsohn tells her patients, "it will assist you in learning to see the connection between your thoughts, feelings, and patterns of behaviors that have plagued you for years." She urges them to write down "anything and everything" in this safe haven.

Susan J. Mendelsohn, *It's Not About the Weight.* Lincoln, NE: iUniverse, 2007, p. 112.

Describing her appearance she says, "My legs were like those of most dancers: a mass of muscles. But the rest of me was skin and bones. My ribcage was completely visible from front to back. My arms looked as though they'd snap, and my face looked way too large for the rest of me."[49]

When she returned home after the summer of strenuous dancing and eating only one meal a day, she was exhausted. Her family and friends were alarmed at her emaciated appearance. Her mother talked of taking her to see a therapist if she did not get back into a normal eating pattern. Lana did not want that to happen so she began to eat a little more and to respond to her hunger rather than to suppress it. Slowly, with the encouragement and support of her family, she began to recover from her anorexia. As her weight increased she found she had more energy for her dancing. Lana realizes that her obsession with being reed thin made her lose control of her life. And she considers herself lucky to have regained that control before it was too late.

Psychotherapy

Lana was able to arrest her anorexia because it was at an early stage and because she had the help of her family. When an eating disorder has been going on for some time, professional help is usually necessary to repair the damage it has done and to arrest it. Psychotherapy is a form of treatment that involves discussions between a therapist and a single patient or a group of patients. It is also known as talk therapy, counseling, or psychosocial therapy.

Individual psychological treatment is most common for adults—especially for those who live alone. Many types of individual therapy are available. A type of talk therapy called cognitive behavioral therapy (CBT) helps the patient identify unhealthy, negative beliefs and behaviors and replace them with healthy, positive ones. It is based on the idea that a person's thoughts, not other people or situations, determine how a person behaves. According to information from the Mayo Clinic, CBT has proven to be beneficial in treating bulimia. It is also used to treat anorexia. However, the Mayo report says no strong evidence proves that it is superior to other forms of therapy used to treat anorexia.

Interpersonal therapy focuses on the person's current relationships with other people. The goal of this therapy is to improve the person's skills in relating to others, including family, friends, and colleagues. The patient learns how to evaluate the way he or she interacts with others and to develop strategies for dealing with relationships and communication problems.

Family therapy is especially important for children or young adults who still live at home. It can help concerned family members learn the best ways to help the patient. It can also resolve family conflicts and uncover family problems that may have been at the root of the eating disorder. Levenkron says family therapy can be a powerful tool for bringing about rapid change in the relationships that foster eating disorders: "[Family therapy] is a setting where often the 'unsayable' (at home) can now be said because a 'referee' is present; a setting where a family can use the therapist as a teacher and role model who can step back, analyze the conflict, and resolve it."[50]

Group psychotherapy is often used in conjunction with individual psychotherapy in both inpatient and outpatient settings. Different groups have different goals. Some groups focus on food, eating, body image, interpersonal skills, and vocational training. Other groups focus on understanding the psychological factors that may have led to the development of the disorder. The participants learn that they are not alone in their struggles. Their interactions (under the guidance of a therapist) include both supporting and confronting each other.

Sharing experiences in a group can be effective in reducing guilt, shame, and a feeling of isolation. Group discussions can also lead to insights about strategies for recovery. A downside to group therapy is the possibility that the youngest members may learn new ways to lose weight. Or, as sometimes happens in a group of anorexics, some may compete to be the thinnest person. However, on the whole, most experts agree that group therapy is usually more beneficial than harmful in treating eating disorders.

During group therapy, participants learn that they are not alone in their struggles. Their interactions (under the guidance of a therapist) include supporting and confronting each other.

Medications

When psychotherapy is not enough to help a patient with anorexia or bulimia, medications may be prescribed. Since depression and anxiety are often components of these diseases, drugs to relieve these symptoms may be used. The goal of the therapist is to keep medications to a minimum.

Depression causes a person to lose the ability to feel joy or to care about his or her present or future life. Severe depression may lead to suicidal impulses. When a person with an eating disorder shows signs of depression, a doctor may recommend an antidepressant. Prozac (fluoxetine) is often prescribed in low doses to help overcome depression.

In addition to relieving the depression, this type of drug has been shown to relieve the need to binge, purge, or starve. A

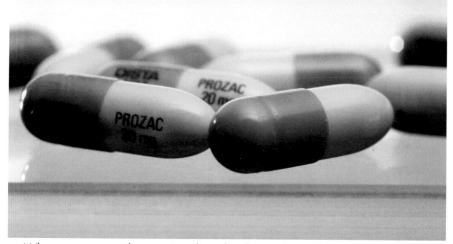

When a person with an eating disorder shows signs of depression, a doctor may recommend an antidepressant such as Prozac.

class of antidepressants called tricyclics increases the level of neurotransmitters such as serotonin in the brain. Research has shown that low levels of serotonin may be responsible for depression and also for the urge to binge or purge.

Anxiety is fear or uneasiness about a coming event. Patients with eating disorders frequently seem to struggle under a heavy load of angst. It may be one of the contributing causes of the eating disorder. And it is likely to increase as the patient worries about undergoing treatment for the disease. Antianxiety drugs can be prescribed to help patients feel calmer. Unfortunately, however, the body develops a tolerance for them, so they become less effective in time.

As happens with many effective but potent drugs, medications used to help patients with anorexia and bulimia can have troublesome side effects. These may include tiredness, confusion, and low blood pressure. Therefore it is important that patients taking them have ongoing medical supervision. Experts agree that medication alone is rarely a solution to recovery from an eating disorder. But in concert with psychotherapy, medication can be helpful.

Animal Therapy

Some therapists are turning to innovative kinds of treatment. David Herzog, an internationally renowned expert on eating disorders, recommends using pets in treating patients. Touch and trust, he says, are very important in the healing process.

Caroline Knapp, one of his patients, has written a memoir, *Pack of Two: The Intricate Bond Between People and Dogs.* Caroline relates her experience with anorexia and the way in which her pets help her stay well. "Put a leash in my hand, put Lucille [her dog] by my side, and something happens, something magical, something clicks inside, as though some key piece of me, missing for years, has suddenly slid into place, and I know I'll be okay."[51]

The use of horses in residential programs is growing in popularity. Remuda Ranch in Arizona was one of the first to use equine therapy in treating eating disorders. Each patient rides two or three times a week on a particular horse. Sharon Simpson, director of Remuda Ranch, says the bond that develops between horse and rider creates a sense of unconditional acceptance that many patients have never experienced before. "Perfection," says Simpson, "does not enter the relationship. The horse is a living breathing animal, and because of that, he can be unpredictable, just like life is unpredictable."[52]

Kacey Cramer is an active worker in the equine therapy field. She traces the beginning of her recovery from fifteen years of nearly fatal anorexia to the day she met a horse named Jake. For Kacey, childhood abandonment and rejection by family members had resulted in a resistance to trusting others. Jake had suffered early physical abuse and also was nervous around strangers. As Kacey and Jake bonded and gave each other unconditional love, she came to feel that it was also possible to trust other people. She worked hard with her treatment team and became open to forming new friendships. Realizing that her motivation to be cured came from her relationship with Jake, she decided to work in the equine-assisted psychotherapy field.

Slips, Lapses, Relapses, Collapses

Despite stories of celebrities who go to rehab centers for a few weeks and emerge cured of their eating disorders, the road to recovery is seldom short or straight. Recovery involves not only physical progress but also emotional healing. After many years of treating patients with eating disorders, Sacker puts the stumbling blocks for patients into four categories: slips, lapses, relapses, and collapses.

Slips are irrational thoughts that originate in the patient's mind. An anorexic patient might have negative thoughts about eating. A bulimic patient might think about what he or she has eaten and about ways to purge it from his or her body. If the pa-

Recovering bulimics may relapse and return to their old habits of bingeing and purging.

tient conceals this kind of irrational thinking and broods on such negative thoughts, they may build up until they lead to a lapse.

A lapse occurs when the patient acts out his or her irrational thinking. It is usually limited and usually brief. But it is scary for the patients and may make them feel as if they are failures. The therapist will try to make the patient understand that lapses are common and are to be expected on the way to recovery.

A relapse is far more serious. It is a return to the eating behavior that made the patient sick. "The difference between a lapse and relapse," says Sacker, "is the difference between a stumble and a bad fall. When you stumble, you can catch yourself in the midst of it; when you fall, you can't stop yourself at all."[53]

With proper treatment the relapse may be turned around. But if it is not checked, it may become a collapse—a full-blown return of the original eating disorder behavior. In fact, it may become an even more intense form of the disorder. Patients sometimes go through more than one cycle of relapse and collapse. They may require medical attention to repair physical damage to their bodies and/or psychiatric care and medication to prevent suicide.

The Long Road to Recovery

Experts agree that no one with severe bulimia or anorexia finds healing neat, orderly, or predictable. Slipping back into old hurtful habits of behavior during treatment and relapses after treatment ends are common. Commenting on celebrities who have been "cured" of an eating disorder, Sacker says, "Actors and models appearing on talk shows make it sound as if getting over an eating disorder is quick and easy, but the reality is very different. Every step of the way is paved with speed bumps, and progress is slow and uneven, with plenty of setbacks."[54]

Michael Strober, director of the Eating Disorder Program at the University of California–Los Angeles (UCLA) Neuropsychiatric Institute, has treated eating disorders for over thirty years. At UCLA, he says, anorexic and bulimic patients are considered recovered "when they maintain a healthy weight and no longer obsessively count calories, binge or purge or manically

How Well Does Treatment Work?

The following estimates of treatment results for eating disorders are from the nonprofit organization Anorexia Nervosa and Related Eating Disorders (ANRED).

The Effectiveness of Treatment for Eating Disorders

- Full recovery after treatment: 60 percent
- Partial recovery after treatment: 20 percent
- No improvement after treatment: 20 percent
- Fatality rate after treatment: 2–3 percent
- Fatality rate without treatment   20 percent

ANRED, quoted in Mark Kittleson, ed., *The Truth About Eating Disorders*. New York: Facts On File, 2005, p. 137.

exercise." Yet even years later these recovered patients show abnormally high rates of anxiety and obsessive thinking, especially perfectionism. "The solution," Strober says, "is not to eliminate these traits but to learn to manage them. So in treatment we try to move patients to a new framework, to enable them to accept growth and change."[55]

When victims of anorexia and bulimia accept the fact that their diseases are controlling their lives and they are willing to make necessary changes, they can hope to overcome them. It is also vitally important for them to learn to recognize and avoid triggers that may cause a reoccurrence. Finding ways to prevent these diseases is the best hope for reducing the number of victims. And fortunately many organizations and specialists are involved in this process.

CHAPTER FIVE

Overcoming Anorexia and Bulimia

The media is constantly raising public awareness about the dangers of eating disorders. Experts appear regularly on programs such as *Oprah Winfrey, Good Morning America, 60 Minutes*, and *Today* to talk about anorexia and bulimia. Because they are forced to explain these complicated diseases in sound bites interrupted by commercials, they often oversimplify. Books and magazine and Web articles written by professionals have more space to explain the complex nature of eating disorders. They also have space to describe the experiences of individuals who have found ways to overcome their disease—even though its ghost may remain to haunt them. For those who are battling eating disorders and for those who are trying to help prevent them, an ever-growing number of resources are available both locally and nationally.

Survival Tactics

Many people who have suffered from acute eating disorders are now happy, productive individuals. They may have had lapses and relapses on the way to recovery. Eventually, however, they have learned ways to cope with the obsessive feelings that still return from time to time. This is especially necessary in times of stress.

Many people who have suffered from acute eating disorders are now happy, productive individuals able to maintain positive relationships with their families.

Nicole, who survived bulimia, says that her recovery was not easy nor completely secure. But during treatment she learned strategies for overcoming the impulses that might trigger a relapse. "There are times even now," she says, "five years later—that I find myself in a food panic. But now, whenever I feel the urge to chow and purge an entire cake, I stop myself and ask, 'Why? Am I really hungry? Or is it because I'm anxious or feeling pressured by something else?'" Each time she makes it safely through the panic attack, her self-confidence grows. She says, "Now I know I'm in charge. Every time I beat that feeling, it's like saying, 'This is my body and my life.'"[56]

Some recovered eating disorder patients compare their survival tactics to changing channels. Gary, who felt pressured to become a pro baseball player, is one who learned to use this method. His obsession with losing weight by not eating and exercising excessively led to full-blown anorexia. Treatment led to his recovery from the disease and to the realization that he was responsible for his actions. "Whenever I'd get the craving to exercise," he says, "I'd go elsewhere—to a different room or out of the house altogether. The important thing was to get my mind off of it. I'd read a book or watch television or go out with a friend."[57]

Joyce Maynard is a writer who became obsessed with her weight and body shape in her late teens. She trained herself to monitor every bite of food that entered her mouth. If she let herself slip and eat a piece of bread or a piece of chocolate, she felt self-hatred and disgust. She convinced herself that food was her enemy.

Then she entered into a relationship with a man who tried to tell her what to eat and how much to eat. She rebelled and started to sneak food. She would binge and then vomit to get rid of the calories. She no longer knew how to eat like a normal person. "I knew only two conditions," she says, "total denial, total indulgence."[58] After becoming a mother, she gradually and painfully learned to eat normally.

Thirty years later the wiring in her brain is still there. She compares herself to an alcoholic who has been sober for thirty years and still speaks of herself as "recovering." "All these years later, in bed at night, I sometimes still run my hand over my ribs, to make sure I can still feel them. I can tell you the exact number of calories in a cashew." She imagines herself getting the flu and throwing up for a couple of days. And she hears an internal radio signal whispering in her ear, "'Oh good, I bet I'll drop four pounds.' I no longer expect," Joyce says, "this voice will ever be silenced entirely. All I can do is take it in, and change the station."[59]

Christy's Story

Christy Heitger-Casbon is a writer on health and fitness, adolescence, and women's issues. In "Back from the Brink," an article in *American Fitness*, she describes how she overcame the obsession with food and weight that nearly killed her.

When she was twelve years old, she drew the conclusion (from family, peers, and the media) that in order to be beautiful and popular, it was necessary to be thin. Within a three-month period she dropped from 110 pounds (50kg) to a skeletal 73 pounds (33.2kg). She was diagnosed with anorexia and landed in a hospital room. Over the next few years she received therapy. After three years she was a healthy weight. But her self-confidence was still very low, and she was still terrified of getting fat.

She did not want to fall back into the starvation routine that led to her anorexia, so she decided to try running as a way of staying thin. At first she hated it, but she kept at it. Then one day she was surprised to find she was actually enjoying it. And she rejoiced as her health improved. Her heart muscle grew stronger, her lung capacity improved, and her body became muscular.

She ran four or five days a week and jogged approximately twenty miles weekly. After a few years, however, her behavior turned unhealthy. She increased the amount of time she exercised until it became an addiction. Even when she experienced knee pain, hip pain, ankle pain, muscle cramps, headaches, shin splints, and pulled muscles, she continued her compulsive running. She panicked when something kept her from exercising. She scheduled business meetings and personal vacations around her running regimen. She even scheduled the time of her wedding around her daily run.

Finally, when she realized that excessive running was controlling her life, she began to gradually alter her behavior. She reduced her mileage and added cross-training activities such as weightlifting, biking, swimming, and tennis. As her new, balanced approach to health and fitness replaced her compulsive behavior, she began to relax and enjoy life more. Christy says, "I have recovered from anorexia and compulsive exercising, but I must remain alert to the start of obsessive behaviors if I am to maintain a healthy lifestyle."[60] Like Christy, everyone who has successfully overcome an eating disorder needs to stay alert for signs that it may be trying to creep back and take control of their lives.

Getting Real

Some celebrities are speaking out against the size zero image as a role model for women. Recently Kate Winslet, the British actress who starred in *Titanic* and won the Oscar for Best Performance by an Actress in a Leading Role 2009 (for her role in *The Reader*) has blasted the idea that a woman has to be thin to be beautiful. Kate has given interviews to magazines and appeared on BBC expressing her views. She is especially critical of the movie industry and the fashion industry for encouraging young girls to aspire to unrealistic body sizes. She emphatically condemns the current fashion trend to wear a size zero.

Kate feels so strongly on the subject that she will not allow magazines containing pictures of super skinny women in her home because she fears they might make the wrong impression on her six-year-old daughter. Kate cites Emma Thompson as an actress who looks like a normal person. And she believes that she herself is an example of the fact that it is not necessary to be thin in order to have a successful career and a happy family life.

In May 2008 twenty-year-old Whitney Thompson was crowned *America's Next Top Model*. Whitney, who is a size ten, was the first ever "full-figured" model to win the competition. As part of her prize package she received a contract with CoverGirl cosmetics and a contract from Elite Model Management. She was also on the cover of *Seventeen* and on a billboard in Times Square.

Actress Kate Winslet speaks openly about her dismay at the unrealistic
size-zero body image that figures so prominently in media images of
girls and women.

Miss America Speaks Out

Kirsten Haglund, Miss America 2008, is one of the celebrities who are working to raise awareness of eating disorders. One of her proactive projects is to get legislation passed that would make sure medical students are educated about these diseases. In her own life, she says she was lucky to have had a doctor who recognized the symptoms. But she cites other cases where emergency room doctors dismissed the symptoms of eating disorders victims as simply being stress or fatigue. Haglund calls pro ana and pro mia sites terrifying. And she contends that anorexia is socially contagious.

Since her win, she has been featured in several national magazines and appeared on *Live with Regis and Kelly, Entertainment Tonight, Extra, E! News,* and other TV shows. Her modeling career is soaring, and she can pick and choose among many offers. She has no intention of becoming skinny. Whitney reports that she has heard from boys and girls all over the world who are dealing with eating disorders. "They're thanking me for standing up and saying, 'I am a plus-size model and I am beautiful.'" And she adds, "*This* is what people look like!"[61]

Guidelines for Fashion Models

In 2007 the Academy for Eating Disorders (an international professional organization concerned with research, treatment, and prevention of eating disorders) issued guidelines aimed at the fashion industry. Their announced goal was to improve the health of fashion models and prevent illness and death resulting from eating disorders. Among the guidelines were these suggestions:

- Adopt an age threshold requiring that models be at least 16 years old.
- For female and male models between 16 and 18 adopt a minimum BMI of 17.4. for women models and 17.7 for male models.

- For women and men over age 18, adopt a minimum BMI threshold of 18.5.
- Adopt a medical-certification requirement that aspiring models do not suffer from an eating disorder and/or related medical complications.
- Develop processes to identify models in need of intervention and refer them to clinicians who can help them.
- Provide educational initiatives for aspiring and working student models, professional models, and their agents and employers to raise awareness of the multiple health risks of low weight and restricted nutritional intake.
- Increase communication with advertising agencies to encourage them to use age-appropriate, realistic models in ad campaigns and reduce unrealistic computer enhancement in preteen and adolescent advertising campaigns.
- Include models of varying weights and body types on both the catwalk and in fashion magazines.[62]

The Academy for Eating Disorders also urged the fashion industry to collaborate with politicians, advertisers, and eating disorder organizations to develop ethical self-regulatory codes and to widen the availability and affordability of eating disorder treatments.

Fighting Deadly Web Sites

The United States has not gone as far as France in legally banning pro–eating disorder Web sites. However, ANAD has published a list of six signs to watch for in recognizing these dangerous sites:

Six Signs of Life-Threatening Eating Disorder Internet Locations

1. Glamorize, reinforce, anorexia nervosa and associated disorders as desirable lifestyles.
2. Focus on weights that are below the generally accepted standards of the medical profession body mass index (BMI).
3. Provide instructions on how to obtain weight reduction

goals through the explanation of diets that are so low in calories these diets are far under accepted standards of nutritionists and health officials.

4. Reinforce behaviors that help eating disorder sufferers to reach weight reduction goals that are harmful and possibly deadly.

5. Provide information on the misuse of drugs in order to induce weight loss through vomiting or bowel movements.

6. Use photos or videos of celebrities, fashion models, or other individual role models who are identified as anorexic.[63]

In 2007 the Academy for Eating Disorders issued guidelines aimed at the fashion industry. At a 2007 London fashion show, a poster is displayed for models with information about getting help.

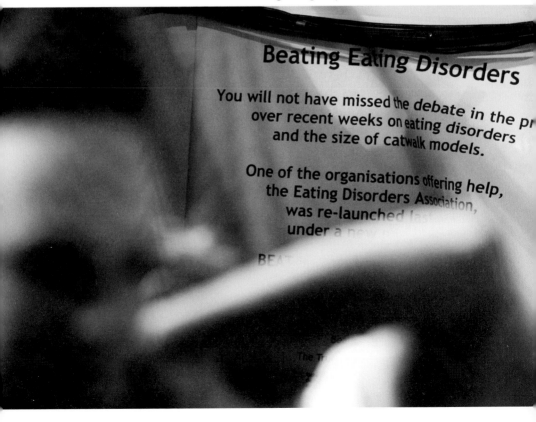

GO GIRLS!

A number of schools across the country have programs designed to make students aware of the dangers of eating disorders. One of the most effective is the NEDA-sponsored GO GIRLS! (Giving Our Girls Inspiration and Resources for Lasting Self-Esteem) program. GO GIRLS! involves high school girls working together to improve their self-esteem and body image while at the same time acting as a voice for change in advertising. The main purpose of GO GIRLS! is to prevent eating disorders. Despite its name, GO GIRLS! does not exclude boys. In fact, some high school boys have made significant contributions to the program. But since 90 percent of eating disorder sufferers are female, the program was created to help them build resistance to these diseases.

Students in the program explore their own body-image issues, learn basic information about eating disorders, and investigate the connection between the media and body image. NEDA says:

> GO GIRLS! teams take an in-depth look at how advertisements are developed, and, in the process, gain an ability to analyze their underlying message. Team members learn how to construct effective letters and presentations to voice their concern to advertisers who either responsibly or irresponsibly impact youth body image. We believe that by becoming "critical viewers" of the media and by discovering effective means of self-expression GO GIRLS! participants will be better able to develop and maintain healthy self-esteem and body image, and in the long run, avoid the devastation of eating problems.[64]

Support Groups

Support groups can be life-saving when their goal is to help members overcome their eating disorders and maintain healthy lifestyles. On the other hand support groups that encourage members to think of their diseases as lifestyles can be deadly. Unfortunately, in addition to the numerous pro ana and pro mia Web sites, this kind of support group is also found in high schools and colleges. In these groups members learn ways to support their illnesses and share tricks to hide them from others.

With a little research, reliable support groups can be found, and most of them are free. Some support groups focus on behaviors that are related to eating disorders. Others deal with underlying emotional issues as well as behaviors. Going to a

Overeaters Anonymous is modeled on Alcoholics Anonymous (AA)—a highly successful self-help group. Like AA, it has a twelve-step program to guide participants to lifelong recovery.

support group for the first time can be a scary experience—especially for a person who has been hiding his or her disease.

Jennie, who suffered from bulimia, describes her first experience of attending a support group recommended by her doctor: "I didn't think I was going to be able to walk through the door. My whole body was shaking. . . . Even though the atmosphere was casual, it was hard to open up at first." Although her story was different from the others in the group, as she listened to them talk she realized they had things in common. "If they were going to make an effort to get over this," Jennie says, "I had no excuse not to try as well."[65]

Overeaters Anonymous (OA) is modeled on Alcoholics Anonymous (AA)—a highly successful self-help group. Like AA it has a twelve-step program to guide participants to lifelong recovery. OA offers special meetings for people with anorexia and bulimia. Some experts find problems with applying the same rules to alcohol addiction and eating disorders. It is unrealistic, they say, to require that the eating disorder patient's behavior stop immediately; a gradual approach may work better. Experts also disagree as to whether the "all or nothing" philosophy of AA works as well with eating disorder patients. However, the OA programs provide a high level of support and fellowship, and many eating disorder patients credit them with helping to overcome their disease.

Resources for Raising Awareness

A number of organizations, including the Academy for Eating Disorders, the American Psychiatric Association, and the Harvard Eating Disorders Center, distribute information about preventing eating disorders. This information is in the form of pamphlets, videos, newsletters, articles in journals, magazines, and on the Web, and also in curricula prepared for use in schools.

NEDA sponsors National Eating Disorders Awareness Week in February. It encourages communities, schools, clubs, and religious groups to hold events designed to make the public more aware of these diseases. Practical help in the form of detailed information for organizers is available from NEDA.

A number of Web sites provide information about where to get treatment for an eating disorder and offer support to those who might be suffering from one.

A number of nonprofit Web sites provide helpful information. Something Fishy is one of the largest, oldest, and most comprehensive Web sites on the topic of eating disorders. It has a detailed treatment finding list (by type of treatment)—for locating treatment centers by country, state, and area code. It has a listing of over eighteen hundred therapists, dieticians, and other professionals who work with victims of eating disorders. It provides in-depth information on these diseases and online peer support forums. The mission statement of Something Fishy reads in part:

We are dedicated to raising awareness about **eating disorders** . . . emphasizing always that eating disorders are **NOT** about food and weight; they are just the symptoms of something deeper going on, inside. Something Fishy is determined to remind each and every sufferer of anorexia, bulimia, compulsive overeating, and binge eating disorder that they are not alone, and that complete **recovery** is possible.[66]

Sharing

Many therapists who are now working in the field of eating disorders have been victims of these diseases themselves. Lindsey Hall is a recovered bulimic. Together with her husband, Leigh Cohn, she has written several books on eating disorders. Lindsey was the first recovered bulimic to appear on national television. Both Lindsey and Leigh have lectured extensively on eating disorders and served as officers of nonprofit eating disorder associations. They are well-known authorities worldwide in the field of eating disorders. Their books have been translated into Japanese, Chinese, Italian, and other languages. Lindsey's understanding of eating disorders has been acquired through long years of close association with these disorders. She says:

> In a perfect world, free from eating disorders, all people would appreciate that love and self-esteem are their birthright regardless of shape or weight. Families, aware of the causes and consequences of eating disorders, would be a constant source of communication and sharing. . . . Food would be a symbol of life rather than a tool for abuse. In other words, people would be allowed to be themselves without conforming to tight-fitting roles based on artificial limits.[67]

Peggy Claude-Pierre is a therapist who has treated and cured hundreds of patients suffering from eating disorders—including her two daughters. In *The Secret Language of Eating Disorders*, she tells the stories of many victims—the ordeal of

The Maudsley Method

A form of family therapy developed by researchers at the Maudsley Hospital in London is receiving worldwide attention. It focuses on patients who are acutely ill with anorexia. In this method the family is seen as the most important resource at the therapist's disposal. The family is not blamed for the illness. Instead, the Maudsley therapist tries to empower the family to assume the responsibility for nurturing their ill child back to health. Despite the fact that this may be frightening to the family, the therapist encourages them with warm acceptance and gives them the expertise to change their child's destructive behavior.

their treatment and the triumph of their recovery. Stacy, one of her patients, says, "The recovery process has not only changed my life but given me a broader understanding of others which has definitely enhanced relationships with family and friends. I now see what a beautiful gift life is. I have been given the chance I thought was lost forever—to live that life."[68]

What better outcome could there be in the battle to overcome eating disorders. How much better it would be, though, if Stacy and the millions who have fought or are fighting similar battles could be spared that ordeal. Without a reduction in the social and cultural emphasis on physical perfection and on thinness as the ideal of that perfection, prevention may be only a wishful dream.

Probably the best hope for a reduction in the numbers of eating disorder victims is through education. Potential victims need to understand the destructive nature of bad eating habits. And they also need to be aware of the numerous helpful resources available to guide them in finding better ways to take control of their lives.

Notes

Introduction: Battling Anorexia and Bulimia

1. Quoted in http://eatingdisorders.about.com/b/2008/06/20/paula-abduls-fight-with-bulimia.htm.

Chapter One: What Are Eating Disorders?

2. Alliance for Eating Disorders Awareness, "Eating Disorders." www.eatingdisordersinfo.org/TypesofEatingDisorder/WhatAreEatingDisorders/tabid/.
3. ANAD, "Facts About Eating Disorders." www.anad.org/223 85/index/html.
4. NEDA, www.nationaleatingdisorders.org/information-resources/general-information.php.
5. Alliance for Eating Disorders Awareness, "Eating Disorders." www.eatingdisorderinfo.org/TypesofEatingDisordersWhatAreEatingDisorders/tabid/.
6. NEDA, www.nationaleatingdisorders.org/information-resources/general-information.php.
7. Christopher G. Fairburn, *Overcoming Binge Eating*. New York: Guilford, 1995, p. 20.
8. MayoClinic.com, "Mental Health: Anorexia Nervosa." www.mayoclinic.com/print/anorexia/D00606/METHOD=print&DSECTION=all.
9. Quoted in Mark J. Kittleson, ed., *The Truth About Eating Disorders*. New York: Facts On File, 2005, p. 70.
10. Quoted in Kathiann M. Kowalski, "Poor Body Image Leads to Anorexia," in *At Issue: Anorexia*, Karen F. Balkin, ed. Detroit: Greenhaven, 2005, p. 74.
11. Quoted in Christina Chiu, *Eating Disorder Survivors Tell Their Stories*. New York: Rosen, 1999, p. 30.
12. MayoClinic.com, "Mental Health: Bulimia Nervosa." www

.mayoclinic.com/print/bulimia/DS00607/METHOD=print&
DSECTION=all.

13. Quoted in GeoCities, "Celebrities with Eating Disorders," p. 1.
www.geocities.com/edpetition/celebritieswitheatdis.html.

14. Quoted in Kittleson, *The Truth About Eating Disorders*, p. 123.

15. "Therapy Analysis – Anorexia and Bulimia." www.pharma
projects.com/therapy_analysis/anorexia-and-bulimia-bu
limia-nervosa.htm.

16. Aimee Liu, *Solitaire*. New York: Harper Colophon, 1980, pp.
49–50.

17. Aimee Liu, *Gaining*. New York: Grand Central, 2008, p.
xxiii.

Chapter Two: Deadly Consequences of Anorexia and Bulimia

18. Quoted in Fred Bronson, *Billboard's Hottest Hot 100 Hits*, Up-
dated and Expanded 3rd Edition*. New York: Billboard Books,
2003, p. 48.

19. Quoted in Scott M. Reid, "Emphasis on Thin Is a Heavy Burden," *GYM Media Report*, January 16, 2005. www.gymmedia
.com/FORUM/agforum/05_01_henrich_e.htm.

20. Quoted in Reid, "Emphasis on Thin Is a Heavy Burden."

21. Quoted in "Celebrities with Eating Disorders," www.geo
cities.com/edpetition/celebritieswitheatdis.html.

22. Quoted in *Starpulse.com*, "Mary-Kate Olsen Says Anorexia
Nearly Killed Her." http://www.starpulse.com/news/index
.php/2008/02/04/mary_kate_olsen_says_anorexia_nearly_kil.

23. Quoted in "Suicides High Among Anorexics." www.eating
disordershelpguide.com./blog/2008/03/suicide-high-among-
anorexics.html.

24. Quoted in Lynette Lamb, "Athletes Are More Vulnerable to
Anorexia than Nonathletes," in *At Issue: Anorexia*, Karen
F. Balkin, ed. Detroit: Greenhaven, 2005, pp. 57–58.

25. Kathleen Tomaselli, "Starving for Perfection: The Changing
Face of Anorexia," *American Medical News*, May 5, 2008.

26. Michael Krasnow, *My Life as a Male Anorexic*. New York:
Harrington Park, 1996, p. 85.

27. Matthew Tiemeyer, "Anorexia and Suicide," quoted in http://eatingdisorders.about.com/od/medicalcomplications/i/suicide_2.htm.

28. Quoted in Peggy Claude-Pierre, *The Secret Language of Eating Disorders*. New York: Vintage, 1999, p. 105.

Chapter Three: Causes of Anorexia and Bulimia

29. Liu, *Gaining*, p. 41.

30. Quoted in Claude-Pierre, *The Secret Language of Eating Disorders*, p. 73.

31. Ira Sacker, *Regaining Your Self*. New York: Hyperion, 2007, pp. 58–59.

32. Susan Mendelsohn, *It's Not About the Weight*. Lincoln, NE: iUniverse, 2007, p. 14.

33. Quoted in Karen F. Balkin, ed., introduction to *At Issue: Anorexia*. Detroit: Greenhaven, 2005, p. 8.

34. Quoted in ANAD, "Eating Disorders and the Internet." www.anad.org/240600/index.html.

35. Kate Taylor, ed., *Going Hungry*. New York: Anchor, 2008, p. xxix.

36. Quoted in GeoCities, "Celebrities with Eating Disorders," p. 1.

37. Ana Cintado, "Eating Disorders and Gymnastics," Vanderbilt University Psychology Department. http://healthpsych.psy.vanderbilt.edu/HealthPsych/gymnasts.htm.

38. Quoted in Ericka Sóuter and Monica Rizzo, "Katharine McPhee's Bulimia Battle," *People*, June 22, 2006. www.people.com/people/article/),1206750,00.html.

39. Sacker, *Regaining Your Self*, p. 162.

40. Fairburn, *Overcoming Binge Eating*, p. 74.

41. Kittleson, *The Truth About Eating Disorders*, p. 45.

42. *Harvard Mental Health Letter*, "Anorexia: An Overview," in *At Issue: Anorexia*, Karen F. Balkin, ed. Detroit: Greenhaven, 2005, p. 13.

43. Quoted in Kate Taylor, ed., *Going Hungry*, pp. 181–82.

44. Steven Levenkron, *Anatomy of Anorexia*. New York: W.W. Norton, 2000, p. 40.

Chapter Four: Treating Anorexia and Bulimia

45. Marya Hornbacher, *Wasted*. New York: HarperPerennial, 2006, pp. 105–6.
46. Ira M. Sacker and Marc A. Zimmer, *Dying to Be Thin*. New York: Warner, 1987, p. 165.
47. Quoted in MayoClinic.com, "Mental Health: Anorexia Nervosa."
48. MayoClinic.com, "Mental Health: Anorexia Nervosa."
49. Lana D'Amico, "Anorexics Lose Control Due to Their Behavior," in *At Issue: Anorexia*, Karen F. Balkin, ed. Detroit: Greenhaven, 2005, p. 71.
50. Levenkron, *Anatomy of Anorexia*, p. 113.
51. Quoted in Liu, *Gaining*, p, 132.
52. Quoted in Liu, *Gaining*, p, 134.
53. Sacker, *Regaining Your Self*, pp. 129–30.
54. Sacker, *Regaining Your Self*, p. 167.
55. Quoted in Liu, *Gaining*, p. 22.

Chapter Five: Overcoming Anorexia and Bulimia

56. Quoted in Chiu, *Eating Disorder Survivors Tell Their Stories*, pp. 50–51.
57. Quoted in Chiu, *Eating Disorder Survivors Tell Their Stories*, p. 33.
58. Quoted in Taylor, *Going Hungry*, p. 297.
59. Quoted in Taylor, *Going Hungry*, p. 301.
60. Christy Heitger-Casbon, "Back from the Brink," *American Fitness*, vol. 18, March 2000, p. 32.
61. Quoted in *Us Magazine*, "Whitney Thompson Named America's Next Top Model," Celebrity News, May 15, 2008. www.usmagazine.com.
62. Quoted in *Psychiatric News*, "New Guidelines Hoped to Reduce Eating Disorders Among Fashion Models," vol. 42, no. 3, February 2, 2007, p. 10. http://pn.psychiatryonline.org /cgi/content/full/42/3/10-a.
63. ANAD, "Eating Disorders and the Internet."

64. "Why Go Girls." www.nationaleatingdisorders.org/p.asp ?WebPage_OD==296.
65. Quoted in Kittleson, *The Truth About Eating Disorders*, p. 136.
66. Something Fishy Web site on Eating Disorders, "Our Mission." www.something-fishy.org.
67. Lindsey Hall and Leigh Cohn, *Bulimia: A Guide to Recovery*. Carlsbad, CA: Gürze, 1999, p. 73.
68. Quoted in Claude-Pierre, *The Secret Language of Eating Disorders*, p. 229.

Glossary

addiction: Physical, emotional, or psychological dependence on something.

anemia: Condition in which the normal number of red blood cells is reduced.

anorexia nervosa: An eating disorder involving intentional starvation.

anxiety: Feelings of fear, worry, and unease.

bingeing: Eating large amounts of food in a short amount of time.

body mass index (BMI): A scale using a person's height and weight to assess level of body fat.

bulimia nervosa: An eating disorder in which a person eats normal or large amounts of food and then rids the body of the food through forced vomiting, abusing laxatives and/or diuretics, taking enemas, or exercising obsessively.

calorie: Measure of energy intake and output in the body.

compulsive exercise (anorexia athletica): A way of purging calories by exercising excessively.

depression: A feeling of hopelessness and sadness.

diuretics: Chemicals used to increase urination and get rid of excess fluid.

eating disorder: An unhealthy, extreme concern with dieting, food, and body image.

gene: The basic carrier of genetic material found in the nucleus of a cell.

lanugo: A covering of soft, fuzzy hair that grows on the face and body of people with severe anorexia.

metabolism: The building-up and breaking-down processes of the body.

nutrients: Substances that provide nourishment for the body.

proteins: Molecules made of amino acids that the body needs to function.

psychiatrist: A medical doctor who is trained to treat people with mental, emotional, and behavioral disorders.

psychology: Science of the mind in any of its aspects.

psychotherapy: Treatment usually based on discussion between patient and doctor or counselor.

remission: A lessening or disappearance of disease symptoms and signs.

self-esteem: Self-respect; confidence in oneself.

serotonin: A chemical thought to be involved in depression and in the control of food intake.

therapy: Treatment or counseling aimed at curing physical or psychological problems.

Organizations to Contact

Alliance for Eating Awareness
PO Box 13155
North Palm Beach, FL 33408-3155
phone: (561) 841-0900
fax: (561) 881-0380
e-mail: info@eatingdisorderinfo.org
Web site: www.eatingdisorderinfo.org

The alliance provides young adults the opportunity to learn about eating disorders and the positive effects of a healthy body image. Distributes educational information to parents and caregivers about the warning signs and dangers of anorexia, bulimia, and other related disorders.

Anna Westin Foundation
112329 Chatfield Ct.
Chaska, MN 55318
phone: (952) 361-3051
fax: (952) 448-4036
e-mail: kitty@annawestinfoundation.org
Web site: www.annawestinfoundation.org

This foundation is dedicated to the treatment and prevention of eating disorders. It is committed to raising public awareness of anorexia and bulimia and to preventing the loss of life through these diseases. Information is available on the Web site.

Anorexia Nervosa and Related Eating Disorders, Inc. (ANRED)
PO Box 5102
Eugene, OR 97405
phone: (503) 344-1144
e-mail: jarinor@rio.com
Web site: www.anred.com

ANRED is a nonprofit organization that provides information about anorexia, bulimia, binge eating, compulsive exercising, and other food and weight disorders, including details about recovery and prevention. ANRED offers workshops, individual and professional training, as well as local community education. It also distributes a monthly newsletter.

Eating Disorder Education Organization (EDEO)
6R20 Edmonton General Hospital
11111 Jesper Ave.
Edmonton, AB T5K 0L4 Canada
phone: (780) 944-2864
e-mail: info@edeo.org
Web site: www.edeo.org

EDEO's primary objective is to increase awareness of eating disorders and their prevalence throughout society. Through education and outreach, the organization encourages people to develop a positive self-image based on ability and personality rather than physical appearance. EDEO publishes a monthly online bulletin and provides speakers to schools and organizations.

Harvard Eating Disorders Center (HEDC)
WACC 725, 15 Parkman St.
Boston, MA 02114
phone: (617) 726-8470
Web site: www.hedc.org

HEDC is a national nonprofit organization. It works to expand knowledge about eating disorders and their detection, treatment, and prevention, and promotes the health of everyone at risk of developing an eating disorder.

**National Association of Anorexia Nervosa
and Associated Disorders (ANAD)**
Box 7
Highland Park, IL 60035
phone: (847) 831-3438

fax: (847) 433-4632
e-mail: info@anad.org
Web site: www.anad.org

ANAD offers hotline counseling, operates an international network of support groups for people with eating disorders and their families, and provides referrals to health care professionals who treat eating disorders. It distributes a quarterly newsletter and information packets and organizes national conferences and local programs. All ANAD services are provided free of charge.

National Eating Disorders Association (NEDA)
603 Stewart St., Ste. 803
Seattle, WA 98101
phone: (206) 382-3587
fax: (206) 829-8501
e-mail: info@nationaleatingdisorders.org
Web site: www.nationaleatingdisorders.org

NEDA is the largest nonprofit organization in the United States working to prevent eating disorders and provide treatment referrals to those suffering from anorexia, bulimia, and binge eating disorders and those concerned with body image and weight issues. NEDA also provides educational outreach programs and training for schools and universities. The organization publishes a prevention curriculum for grades four through six as well as public prevention and awareness information packets, videos, guides, and other materials.

For Further Reading

Books

Carrie Arnold, *Next to Nothing*. New York: Oxford University Press, 2007. This book is an insightful account of a teenager's experience and recovery from an eating disorder.

Sandra Augustyn, ed., *Eating Disorder Information for Teens*. Detroit: Omnigraphics, 2005. This book contains basic information about anorexia, bulimia, binge eating, and other eating disorders. It includes useful information for teens on how to stay healthy.

Karen F. Balkin, ed., *At Issue: Anorexia*. Detroit: Greenhaven, 2005. This book includes articles that provide information on anorexia from a variety of perspectives. It includes an annotated list of relevant organizations to contact for information and an extensive bibliography for further research.

Mark J. Kittleson, ed., *The Truth About Eating Disorders*. New York: Facts On File, 2005. This book presents facts and information on the various kinds of eating disorders. Topics discussed include causes of eating disorders, how to recognize signs of eating disorders, obesity and weight control, and relevant subjects.

Aimee Liu, *Gaining*. New York: Hachette, 2008. In this book Liu recalls her struggles with eating disorders and explores current research on these diseases. She discusses innovative treatments and ways to prevent developing eating problems.

Susan J. Mendelsohn, *It's Not About the Weight: Attacking Eating Disorders from the Inside Out*. Lincoln, NE: iUniverse, Inc., 2007. Mendelsohn is a doctor of clinical psychology who specializes in treating eating disorders. In this book she shares her personal story of recovery from an eating disorder and information about the causes of eating disorders. Out of her experience with these diseases she offers useful advice.

Ira M. Sacker, *Regaining Your Self*. New York: Hyperion, 2007. In this book Sacker, an eating disorders expert, offers useful information on recognizing the early warning signs of eating disorders and on penetrating the mixed messages that patients may present. He uses his thirty-five years of experience to untangle some of the mystery surrounding these diseases.

Maria Stavrou, *Bulimics on Bulimia*. London: Jessica Kingsley, 2009. This book is a collection of accounts by people who are living with bulimia. It reveals the complex realities of the illness and the different ways in which different people view themselves and their disorder. And it sheds new light on the day-to-day struggle of victims of the disorder.

Kate Taylor, ed., *Going Hungry*. New York: Anchor, 2008. In this book nineteen writers describe their experiences with eating disorders. Their powerful stories shed light on many facets of eating disorders such as anxiety, depression, fashion, family, genetics, sexuality, and sports.

Web Sites

GO GIRLS! (Giving Our Girls Inspiration and Resources for Lasting Self-Esteem) (www.nationaleatingdisorders.org /asp?WebPage_ID=296). GO GIRLS! sponsors a high school prevention program and curriculum that involves high school girls working together to improve self-esteem and body image while acting as a voice for change in advertising by major retailers in the media.

The Gürze Books Eating Disorders Web site (www.gürze .com). This site includes over 150 books on eating disorders and related topics with photos and annotations, video and audiotapes, links to treatment facilities, nonprofit organizations, and other related information sites.

The Mirror-Mirror Website on Eating Disorders (www .mirror-mirror.org/eatdis.htm). This site provides definitions, signs, and symptoms; physical dangers; specific information on athletes, men, and children with eating disorders; relapse warning signs; and more. It also has links to many personal Web sites of individuals who now have or have recovered from eating disorders.

Something Fishy (www.something-fishy.org). This site is dedicated to increasing awareness of eating disorders and encouraging recovery. It provides information and online support links to other sites, chat rooms, guest speakers, and much more.

Index

A
Abdul, Paula, *11*, 11–12
Academy for Eating Disorders, 79, 80
Alliance for Eating Disorders Awareness, 13, 16
American Journal of Psychiatry, 51
American Medical News (newspaper), 38
American Psychiatric Association, 59
ANAD (National Association of Anorexia Nervosa and Associated Disorders), 15–16, 80
Anatomy of Anorexia (Levenkron), 54
Animal therapy, 68–69
Anorexia, 8–10
  diagnosis of, 59–60
  difficulty of recovery from, 54–55, 69–71
  gene mutation identified in, 53
  meaning of, 15
  symptoms of, 17–18
  treatment of, 60–61
Anorexia Nervosa and Related Eating Disorders (ANRED), 72

B
Barbi, Shane, 34–35
Barbi, Sia, 34–35
Becker, Anne, 46
Beckham, Victoria, 47, *48*
Binge, 15
Binge eating disorder (BED), 15, 16

Black women, 20
Body image/self-esteem
  challenges to, 44–46
  media messages and, 43
Body mass index (BMI), 33, 79–80
Bulimia, 10–12
  diagnosis of, 61–62
  meaning of, 15
  symptoms of, 21–23
  treatment of, 62–63

C
Carpenter, Karen, 29–30, *31*, 32
Chisholm, Melanie, 47, *48*
Cholecystokinin (CCK), 54
Cintado, Ana, 49
Claude-Pierre, Peggy, 40, 86–87
Cognitive behavioral therapy (CBT), 65–66
Cohn, Leigh, 86
Cortisol, 54
Cramer, Kacey, 69
Crow, Scott, 38

D
D'Amico, Lana, 64–65
Depression
  eating disorders and, 16, 53
  treatment of, 67
Dying to Be Healthy (Barbi and Barbi), 35
Dying to Be Thin (Sacker), 59

E
Eating disorders
  among athletes/performers, 49

101

Picture Credits

About the Author

Elizabeth Silverthorne is the author of more than twenty books for children and adults, plus numerous articles and short stories. Her father and her husband were physicians. Her daughter is a microbiologist. Silverthorne lives in Salado, in the heart of Texas.